Organizational
Analysis:
A Sociological
View

3.95

Behavioral Science in Industry Series

Edited by Victor H. Vroom
Yale University

☐ = //

Organizational Analysis: A Sociological View

Charles B. Perrow
The State University of New York at Stony Brook

Brooks/Cole Publishing Company
Belmont, California

Tavistock Publications, Ltd.
London

L. C. Cat. Card No.: 70–98404
Printed in the United States of America

5 6 7 8 9 10–74

Published simultaneously in Great Britain by Tavistock Publications, Ltd.

foreword

The heterogeneity of behavioral science in industry makes it impossible for a single author to do justice to the subject's many facets in a single text. Although full-length volumes on particular topics are available for the specialist, these books are often beyond the level of the advanced undergraduate or beginning graduate student, and they typically go into more detail than is justified in a general course. To meet the changing educational needs generated by this complex subject matter, the Behavioral Science in Industry series was conceived.

The concept is simple. Leading authorities have written short books, at a fairly basic level, to present the essentials of particular fields of inquiry. These books are designed to be used in combination, as a basic text for courses in industrial psychology or behavioral science in industry, or singly, as supplementary texts or collateral reading in more specialized courses.

To implement this concept, the editor outlined the general scope of the series, specified a list of titles, and sketched the content of each volume. Leading social scientists nominated authors for each of the proposed books, and, in following up these leads, the editor was extremely fortunate in enlisting the enthusiastic cooperation of the kinds of men who are not only specialists in their subjects, but who can communicate their ideas in highly readable fashion.

The need for such a series is apparent from the marked changes that have occurred in the last two or three decades in the application of the scientific method to the study of human behavior at work. Perhaps the most significant of these changes is the extension of the range of problems subjected to systematic research. The continuing concern of industrial psychology with methods of assessing individual differences for the selection and placement of personnel has been supplemented by intensive research on such diverse topics as leadership and supervision, the design of man-machine systems, consumer preferences, management development, career patterns, and union-management relations.

This expanding focus of industrial psychology has been accompanied by changes in the objectives and strategies of research. Research has become less concerned with techniques for solving particular problems and more concerned with shedding light on the processes that underlie various behavioral phenomena, on the assumption that improvements in technology will be facilitated by a better understanding of these processes. To implement these new objectives, the psychometric and correlational methods of research in personnel selection and placement were adapted to new problems and supplemented by experiments in laboratory and field settings. As a result, the study of behavior in industrial organizations has been undertaken by researchers who have not previously been identified with industrial psychology. Experimental psychologists investigated problems of human factors in equipment design; social psychologists worked on problems of leadership, communication, and social influence; and clinical psychologists applied their diagnostic and therapeutic skills in industrial settings.

The net effect has been a blurring of the boundary lines among these subdisciplines and a growing recognition of the interdependence of "basic" and "applied" research. These changes have also obscured lines of demarcation among disciplines and professions. Psychologists, sociologists, cultural anthropologists, political scientists, and economists, and specialists in such functional managerial fields as production, labor relations, marketing, and accounting have discovered that much of their work is interrelated and that their interests are often mutual. The resultant cross-fertilization has given an interdisciplinary character to much of the new research and has afforded some currency to the interdisciplinary label *behavioral science*.

This series has been planned to reflect these changes in subject matter and research methods and to provide the reader with a valuable summary of the current status of behavioral science in industry.

Victor H. Vroom

preface

This book is intended for those who need to know something about organizational behavior in order to manage, or survive in, organizations. Most of the organizational literature they read is social-psychological and heavily oriented toward leadership problems and human relations. In contrast, I have relied upon a sociological approach and emphasized organizational structure, goals, and environment. In working with a variety of organizations it has been my experience that manipulating the structure, analyzing the goals, and grasping the nature of the environment are more practical and efficient ways of dealing with organizational problems than trying to change human behavior directly, and that is the essential argument of the book.

Attempting to make sociological theory relevant for practicing managers has meant that several standard topics on the subject—generally those without much relevance—are excluded. On the other hand, some topics that are only lightly touched upon in most sociological texts are treated in considerable detail, particularly organizational goals and the environment. Thus, though the book is not explicitly addressed toward sociologists, I think they will profit from it; it is surprising how much discipline is imposed upon theory by requiring that it "make a difference" and provide guidance or useful illumination. I learned long ago from students in professional schools that questions of "so what" or "what relevance does this have" do not signify impatience with theory *per se*, much less anti-intellectualism, but only impatience with the obvious, general, remote, and vague statements that often parade as social science theory. One test of good theory is that it have practical implications; I hope there will be such benefits here.

Relevant theory, however, is not the same as useful techniques, and there is little here about specific techniques. What good theory does is show how to analyze an organization or an organizational problem so that judicious selections of specific techniques can be made. If the costs of a particular unit have gotten out of line, for instance, one should be able to analyze the problem so as to choose among the various remedies available—better cost accounting, budget slashing, or whatever. There are appropriate techniques for accomplishing each of these remedies, but the prior problem is to define one's goals and the source of the difficulty. That involves conceptualizing the organization and the role of the particular unit, and, for that, sociological theory is essential. Thus, the major theoretical thrust of this book is to provide conceptual tools, and the conceptual tools required by the practicing manager are the same as those required of theory builders and academic researchers.

Since conceptualization—ways of looking and seeing—should not proceed in a vacuum, I have made a considerable effort to include descriptive and anecdotal material. One might even gather that I spend most of my time reading company stories in *Fortune*. (If there were a counterpart magazine for hospitals, social agencies, and government agencies, perhaps called *Debt*, I would have used more illustrations from those fields. As it is, I have tried to include, at each step, examples from nonprofit organizations, also.) A good way to discipline theory is to relate it to descriptions made for other purposes, even though this is often considered mere "illustration." Furthermore, I know no better way to present the flavor of organizational life than by dealing with actual organizations.

I have taken the position that controversy, off-hand criticisms, and casual comments about colleagues and disciplines can only enliven a field that has been excessively dull. We perpetrate a myth that all social scientists march hand-in-hand down a single road toward the truth. But when students are not looking we squabble among ourselves; make uncharitable asides which never get published; and rush, stumble, or casually stroll down a variety of roads that often go nowhere and mostly come back to where we started.

Although I have tried to insert a great deal of this irreverent and perhaps irrelevant flavor into this book, much was unfortunately edited out on the advice of misguided but well-meaning friends. Still, there is a substantial residue, and I trust few minds will be poisoned by it.

The first chapter is based on the assumption that the reader will know little of the sociological perspective, but that if he has read anything representative in the area of organizational behavior, he will have two firmly established prejudices that must be shaken. The most important prejudice, which will be dealt with at length, is that organizational problems are people problems, and that good leadership is the answer. The second, minor prejudice is that current work in psychology, social psychology, and sociology has demolished classical management theory and replaced it with new and true principles. I try to show that many people problems and leadership problems are really due to organizational structure and that while classical management theory is quite deficient, it does deal with important problems that the other approaches neglect. Having jarred, hopefully, these two views, I then cast a critical eye on my own discipline.

Chapter Two makes a simple point at length: organizations differ widely, and thus what purports to be true of all of them is likely to be either exceedingly general or very trivial. Detailed illustrations are given, for I have found that this simple truth is difficult to grasp and is frequently ignored in the search for the "one best way." The point is demonstrated by contrasting organizations where routine tasks predominate with those that have nonroutine tasks.

The distinction between routine and nonroutine tasks revealed in Chapter Two becomes a comparison of highly bureaucratized and less bureaucratized organizations in Chapter Three. This chapter examines the occasion for structure, or bureaucratization, in organizations and explores the basis for differing degrees of structure. Utilizing the concept of technology, problems of mixing different degrees of structure are discussed. More complex models, which describe three or four types of firms, are presented next. The goal is to give the student tools that will allow him to analyze the specific nature of a single organization, and thus to select management techniques more carefully.

These first three chapters thus deal with the structure and functioning of organizations, concentrating upon internal matters. But sociologists have also examined two other important and difficult areas—the influence of the environment on organizations and the nature of organizational goals. The environment is considered in Chapter Four. Since we lack a unifying theory in this area, it is a discourse in a general way about some matters of which the average student is likely to be quite unaware. ranging from culture to trade relations men. This chapter not only offsets the preoccupation of most books with internal dynamics, but tries to warn the student about some peculiar phenomena he will encounter that stem from relationships with outside groups.

Chapter Five deals with the messiest problem of all—but the one to which all analytical roads should lead: the nature of organizational goals and the strategies used to achieve them. This chapter romps through some fascinating case histories illustrating the variety of goals pursued by business firms (goals of which even the well informed reader may be unaware), and the varying strategies utilized. Hopefully, the discussion will provide the reader with a greater understanding of the complexity of the organizational world and some incentive to analyze—and perhaps seek to change—the goals of organizations with which he may be associated.

Finally, the last chapter wraps up the subject in some pleasant generalities and some urgent admonitions.

Charles Perrow

acknowledgments

In our handsomely subsidized world of research and writing few of us can claim to have written a book completely on our own time and with our own paper. It is very difficult to allocate costs and thus to parcel our gratitude with scrupulous honesty. But there is no doubt that the largess of the Wisconsin Alumni Research Foundation of the University of Wisconsin, wisely distributing the royalties from a pesticide, has helped materially.

If this book should please the reader, it would be well to re-read this paragraph concerning a few of the people who have enriched the work. If the book should displease, forget it; it is not their fault. First, the perspective stems from the work of my former teacher, Philip Selznick, professor of sociology, University of California, Berkeley, who never pursued organizational analysis as an end in itself. I owe more to James D. Thompson, professor of sociology at Vanderbilt University, than his scrutiny of some early drafts of the first chapters; no one else has pursued the subject of organizational environment to more effect, and he was the first to dabble in technology, as the word is used here. Many improvements are also due to a careful critical reading by George Strauss, professor of business administration, University of California, Berkeley. Finally, my wife, Edith, raised more questions about the initial drafts of this volume than either of us cares to remember; I took her suggestions very seriously, like the model husband that I am.

contents

chapter
one

Perspectives
on Organizations

No matter what you have to do with an organization—whether you are going to study it, work in it, consult for it, subvert it, or use it in the interest of another organization—you must have some view of the nature of the beast with which you are dealing. This constitutes a perspective on organizations.

The purpose of this book is to present a distinctive viewpoint regarding complex organizations and to make a frankly imperialistic case for this perspective. By setting it off against other viewpoints, especially in this first chapter, I wish to highlight its distinctiveness. I don't expect the other viewpoints to dry up and wither away; if anything, *their* virtues should become even more distinct after I have had my say.

Because all viewpoints are limited, their value lies in the particular camera-angle which is selected. One is used to reveal one implication, another to explore a different problem. The clinical psychologist catches the executive in a closeup, exploring the tensions of his aggressive personality. The social psychologist cuts from the executive to the members of his staff, illuminating the uncertainties of status and the waning cohesion of the group as the time approaches to choose a new president. The administrative theorist stands back and coolly assesses the discrepancy between the responsibilities and the authority of a subordinate, a gap never calculated by an executive who has cluttered up his communication channels. The economist inserts a wide-angle lens and comments that the market has dropped, while the political scientist notes that labor is in control of the legislature.

There is room for all these viewpoints, depending upon whether the analyst wishes to understand the personality of the executive, the function of the group, the administrative design of the organization, or some other special facet. Those who take a social-structural viewpoint, however, are likely to eschew most of these approaches. They are interested in the organization *per se*—in the enduring patterns of behavior that give it its form and structure. Most analysts at the present time are likely to look at the group bases of power of the executive team members, the typical "routes to the top," the interaction of organizational history and competencies on the one hand, and the changing environment on the other, to explain this scene. They will draw from the other perspectives, but the organizational explanation of organizational behavior is their paramount consideration.

In this chapter we will contrast the prevailing view of organizations —an emphasis upon "people problems" and "leadership" problems— with the structural emphasis. Briefly, the structural viewpoint considers the roles people play, rather than the nature of the personalities in these roles. It deals with the structures in which roles are performed—the relationship of groups to each other, such as sales and production; the .degree of centralization or decentralization; and the "climate" of values and expectations and goals in the organizations—something which will occasionally be referred to as the "character" of the organization. The sociologist also takes an "open system" point of view. That is, he examines, for example, the way the organization is influenced by its environment; the impact of new sources of personnel recruitment on the structure and values of the organization; the role of technology in changing the structure and goals of the organization. These "open system" characteristics are discussed chiefly in subsequent chapters.

In this initial chapter we shall also examine the structural view of an approach somewhat similar to the sociological one—the much denigrated approach of classical management theory, or "scientific management." Finally, some of the conceptual and methodological limitations of the sociological viewpoint will be considered. Like all perspectives, it has its traps, and the student is best forewarned about them.

"Organizations Are People"

One of the enduring truisms of organizational analysis is that organizations are, after all, made up of people. Such a statement usually brings about a sagacious nodding of heads and a comfortable feeling of being on solid ground. But it is also true that organizations are inanimate things—they are filing cabinets, typewriters, machinery, records, mailing lists, or goods and services. This observation usually elicits no resounding thump on the table. Still, it raises a good question. Why are we so determined to equate organizations with people? It appears, at first glance at least, that most of the problems of organizations do arise from the people within them. In a simpler period of history this probably was less true. Mechanical devices were imperfect and problems of capital, land, and labor markets predominated. People were largely taken for granted and "leadership" was not the elusive and vital resource that it seems to be today. Leadership required only strong will and a few relatively simple ideas—at least in contrast to the complexity of modern organizations. Today, in organizations as well as in society in general, as Riesman (63) has told us, our problems are people problems—interpersonal relations—rather than the material conditions of life and the concrete machinery of organizations.

People in this view, then, are the source of the problem, so this is the way organizations are defined. Furthermore, people can be changed or at least selected, whereas many other aspects of organizations seem to be beyond control. It is quite obvious what is wrong with people when they do things wrong. Jones is too conservative; Smith doesn't delegate authority; Brown is out only for himself. On these matters we are all experts. It is less simple, or rather it is a problem for specialists only, to determine what is wrong with the capital structure of the firm where Jones appears too conservative, or the psychiatric techniques employed in a mental hospital where Dr. Smith acts so dictatorially, or the uncertain political structure of the governmental bureau where Brown keeps shifting his alliances.

So let us alter the truism to say that visible organizational problems generally are exemplified by the people in the organizations and their relationships with one another. But this does not necessarily mean that in order to change these problems you have to change the people. For example, one of the persistent complaints in the field of penology, or juvenile correctional institutions, or mental hospitals, or any of the "people-changing" institutions is the need for better workers. Their problems, we hear, stem from the lack of high-quality personnel. More specifically, the types of individuals they can recruit as guards, or cottage parents, or orderlies typically have too little education, hold oversimplified views about people, tend to be punitive, and believe that order and discipline can solve all problems. Undoubtedly many with such attitudes work in prisons and hospitals just as there are many such people in steel mills, IBM, the Bureau of the Budget, universities, and all other types of organizations.

But sociologists challenge this view by arguing that people's attitudes are shaped at least as much by the organization in which they work as by their preexisting attitudes. The very real constraints and demands presented by the job may dictate behavior which we call punitive; then we call the *person* punitive. In one study (55) a number of applicants for positions as low-level supervisors in a juvenile correction institution were asked in an anonymous questionnaire about their opinions on the causes of delinquency, how delinquents should be handled, what was really wrong with delinquents, and whether or not they really differed much from other kids. The applicants' attitudes on the whole turned out to be quite enlightened and permissive. Some were subsequently hired by the institution, and after they had worked for a while they were again queried, as were all other personnel in the institution. It was found that the recent employees' opinions had markedly changed, and they now shared the views of the other personnel. They had become less permissive and took a punitive, unenlightened view regarding the causes of delinquency and the care and handling of delinquents. Thus, they had adopted the very attitudes about which the heads of these institutions had complained—only these were not the views they had brought with them. Considering the meager techniques for changing the character of delinquents, there was really little opportunity for the staff to do anything but adjust to the realities of the organization and the way it was run. Then they altered their attitudes to conform to the behavior expected of them. The truism "organizations are people" is not much use in analyzing the problems of this institution.

It is difficult to change people directly through training programs and other psychological means; a good deal of backsliding is likely. Thus we will explore in this book other possible remedies which might change people, or, more accurately stated, which would bring out different facets in people. It may not be the best strategy to argue that, since old Joe has a pretty tidy mind and is good with details, let us move him over to accounting and take him out of sales where imagination is needed. This may be true, but the question which should be asked first is whether sales is so organized that the only way Joe can get along there is by focusing on details. Might it not be true that if the organizational

structure of the sales department, or its place in the company p
structure, or the techniques it uses, were changed, then neither Jc
anybody else would be concerned with detail but would be free to
summon up initiative and imagination? Otherwise, you might put
young Bill in there with all his initiative and imagination, and in a few
years he would begin to look like old Joe. This is not to suggest that the
many treatises on personnel selection are thus easily dismissed. The
better ones note that it may be necessary to alter the structure of an
organization and to redefine tasks because supermen are in short supply.
Still, there is more to an organization than its people. It is clear that
"organizations are people" is a shotgun approach to organizational
problems—the target and the weapon are unselective.

"It's a Matter of Leadership"

"The critical thing in organizations is the kind of leadership."
"Leaders summon the appropriate qualities of men." "Without good
leadership nothing is possible." "The trouble with this organization is
that it lacks good leadership." The phrases are as popular in executive
boardrooms as they are in textbooks, and new types of "leadership styles"
are coined each year in academic research.

Obviously there is some substance in this rather more sophisticated
approach. We have all seen people in leadership positions who are poor
leaders and some who are good leaders. But the attempt to discover those
traits that would identify future leaders or to determine the common
characteristics of good leaders has been frustrating, even though it has
occupied a great deal of the time of social scientists and those in business
administration. Careful studies which meet the minimal criteria of
scientific objectivity generally find that leadership is specific to the
circumstances and the tasks demanded of the leader. In some situations,
to use one current formulation, the best leader is one who exercises
human relations skills; in other situations it is the technical expert; and
in still others it is the planner and organizer. "Findings indicate that
leadership in the formal organization is a highly relative process, with
different combinations of supervisory-leadership skills and practices
being required at different levels of supervision in the same organization
and at different times in the life of an organization" (40, p. 103). This
sounds like a dull generalization, but if you had followed for 15 or 20

years the tortuous evolution of this apparently simple idea you would have shared in some genuine intellectual excitement. Tested ideas are hard to come by.

Defining the situations which need one or the other type of leadership clearly is the next step, and then we are in sociological territory. For it is quite possible to put a man in a position where he is trained for, and rewarded for, exercising human relations skills when he should be planning and directing. Of course, in some kinds of circumstances more than one method can succeed; leaders with quite different traits or characteristics can do well in such a job. What types of situations are these? The sociological answer is that leadership style is a "dependent variable" which depends upon or follows from something else. The setting or task is the "independent variable": that which is independently determined by something else causes the variation in the dependent factor. This can be illustrated by the fascinating history of one of the research centers which has investigated leadership more than any other through "empirical" means, that is, through questionnaires, interviews, and observation techniques which can be quantified and replicated.

The Institute for Social Research at the University of Michigan, established shortly after the end of World War II, included a group of persons concerned with the study of organizations. Arnold Tannenbaum and Stanley Seashore recently paused and took a long look at the changes in their research direction over a 15-year period. They noted that the initial attempts to understand human relations problems in organizations were focused upon the rank-and-file members. As psychologists, they viewed organizations as collections of people. They believed that human problems in organizations were obviously problems of individuals. Also, their research in many cases was supported by contracts from private companies whose heads tended to attribute their problems to people in lower organizational ranks.

The first problem they encountered a few years later was that they could not prove the obvious hypothesis that satisfied workers were more productive than unsatisfied workers. They found no consistent differences between satisfaction in high- and low-producing work groups; in some cases the least satisfied workers were the highest producers. Findings of this sort, which contradicted the obvious hypotheses, repeatedly emerged. So they began to look at the characteristics of the supervisor and of the work group as a whole. Here their efforts were more fruitful. As they summarize it, "supervisors of high-producing groups seem in the workers' view to behave differently than supervisors of low-producing groups; they seemed to be different kinds of people. In many cases the high-producing supervisor was less punitive towards his subordinates, he supervised in general ways rather than closely, he was more likely to be concerned about his subordinates as human beings, as individuals, rather than as means for turning out a product" (79, p. 5). It mattered little whether workers were satisfied with their jobs; what did matter was the way the supervisor behaved.

But how could these findings be applied? As psychologists, they believed at first that the obvious application was through leadership training. However, they found that supervisors were "quick to learn right from wrong in the classroom situation but it was another matter back on the shop floor." There the circumstances were inconsistent with the principles of good supervision. It then appeared that the structure of the organization established processes that might be the source of variance. They note: "Our present approach thus implies a more wholistic conception of organizations. . . . In some respects this applies to a sociological as well as a psychological definition of the problem. It has become unmistakably clear that the behavior of people in organizations cannot effectively be studied from a psychological viewpoint, traditionally defined" (79, pp. 1–2).

This conclusion is pleasant to hear from psychologists. Still, Tannenbaum and Seashore and their associates continue to fall short of a structural view of organization. As they see it, the organizational task is to persuade supervisors to respect their men. The way to do this, they say, is to change the organization to give the men some authority, responsibility, influence, and control over significant aspects of their work life. As laudable as this goal may be in terms of the individual, it still remains a circumscribed definition of the problem of organizational analysis. (Of course, the psychologist's interests differ to some extent from those of a sociologist, who is more concerned with understanding rather than with improving organizations.) Their approach still leans heavily upon training the whole organization from top to bottom, as they explicitly indicate. But it is not necessarily poor training which created the problems, and retraining may not touch them. The source of difficulty may lie in the market situation, in history, in tradition, in the structure of incentives, or in technology, among others. By focusing upon supervisory relations they miss the larger picture, some part of which may have a great deal more to do with organizational behavior than poor training.

A Case of Sales Domination

Let me give a concrete illustration of an organizational problem that was almost universally defined as a leadership difficulty to be corrected by changing a man's behavior, but that could be equally well-defined as a problem in what is sometimes called "organizational character" (69).

The organization was an industrial firm employing close to 2,000 people in one location. The individual in question was a Mr. Strong, the vice-president of production. He had been promoted from within and was well known for his ambition, technical competence, hard work, and drive. Strong was a no-nonsense manager, somewhat isolated, socially, from the other corporate officers. People generally felt that he was unable to delegate authority. He insisted on reviewing every detail, and he "contracted" a great deal more than was necessary (dipped down into the lower levels of his organization to give direct orders). He was also criticized because he would not give an accurate picture of production problems to the other vice-presidents.

Sales, for example, found that when they wished to know the status of an order they had to check two or three sources for information because they were given conflicting statements. This situation was attributed to Mr. Strong's contracting behavior. Communication problems extended even to production's unwillingness to admit mistakes or to indicate how extensive delays might be. Again, Mr. Strong's personal characteristics were blamed. He ran a tight ship and kept a closed mouth. It was said that he would be a good leader in a much larger organization where he was not functioning at a vice-presidential level.

Our own analysis suggested that while some of his behavior might have been related to his own peculiarities, this was not certain, and in fact there was little suggestion of these personality problems before he became vice-president of production. Nor did he seem to be the type who would respond to, or even tolerate, leadership training or "T-group" therapy (sensitivity training). In any case, it was worthwhile to explore other interpretations. The one we arrived at was associated with a marked characteristic of this company—it had always been dominated by sales personnel. Most of the top executives had come up through sales; this was perceived by personnel as the quickest and perhaps the only route to the top. Sales, it was generally admitted, called the shots and got the rewards. The ambitious Mr. Strong, however, was in production.

In a company with a strong sales unit run by those who were sales-bred and -oriented, production had little representation in top policy circles. In fact, some strong men at or near the top of the production hierarchy had been forced out of the company in the past. Production was operating against overwhelming odds. But what had worked well in the past had become inappropriate, for the company was no longer producing easy-to-make items where the major problem was selling them, but hard-to-make items which were easy to sell if the quality was high. Production was now more important than sales.

Fortunately for the company, Mr. Strong was a strong individual and did not intend to crumble under this pressure. He appeared to have evolved a useful scheme for meeting the pressure. He had concluded that it was important that the vice-president of production be the key link in all possible exchanges of information no matter how small, so that he would have a ready explanation for any problems which might arise. Thus he warded off contacts between his production staff and sales personnel, protected production from excessive criticism from sales people, and prevented the release of information that might be critical of production. But his techniques also led to his taking over many of the functions of middle management, thus weakening his organization. Every sales demand appeared to create a crisis. As a result, in the interest of speed, the vice-president had to bypass people directly under him and give orders to persons further down in the organization.

In this situation, a supervisor might know less about what was going on than the man under him. Realizing this, sales had to query the production hierarchy at several levels because of the conflicting information received from their personnel. The crisis atmosphere produced by the demands of sales (they were used to having their way) also prevented long-range planning which might have helped correct specific problems. As long as the sales people set up a clamor, it did no good to send Mr. Strong pamphlets on the virtue of planning ahead. In a company like this, where the vice-president of sales maintains that, "It is up to production to conform," production risks less by trying to meet a delivery date or trying to make a product than it risks by refusing to try. To refuse to try is to admit to inadequacy, reinforcing sales' criticisms. To try is to conform, even if you fail. Hence, production appeared to have unrealistic optimism and expectations. Since their performance was judged in terms of their support of sales, they must, at least on the surface, agree to sales' demands, however unrealistic.

Nor would production's image be enhanced if they were frank

about their difficulties. Most of their problems concerned scheduling, excessive overtime work, overloading of facilities, special orders, lack of process research, and rushing into new projects. Sales department demands were the cause. In top-management meetings, however, the vice-president of production could not openly challenge sales domination so he attributed his problems to such generalities as inadequate equipment, poor materials, or customer misuse of the products. Of course, these excuses did not satisfy sales.

The morale of the managers in production was severely damaged, as a result. The area of their authority was reduced by the contracting behavior of the vice-president; their problems were not realistically discussed by top management; they were always on the defensive with sales; and all the organization's difficulties were attributed to production personnel in formal meetings and informal statements.

We have already seen that the problems of the company were actually due to the excessive domination of a sales perspective. With the plant running at excess capacity, the problems of production were greatest, and it was not the time for sales to call all the shots. Had the pressure been taken off the vice-president of production it might have developed that he could now *afford* to delegate and engage in more long-range planning, could be more frank about his problems, and seek the cooperation of sales. No training program could bring this about. A wholesale change in the character of the company was necessary. Production would have to be seen as a viable route to the presidency. Talented people should not have been expected to jump into sales as soon as they could in order to find rewards for their talents. The perspective of middle and top management should have been adjusted away from overemphasis on sales. Salesmen should have been encouraged occasionally to cite longer delivery times or to change their unrealistically low prices for special orders. There is no need for a detailed discussion of the character of this company and how it would have to change. But these facts are sufficient to show that what appears to be a leadership problem or a training problem may actually be a sociological problem when one examines the nature of the organization as a whole.

In sum, we have seen that apparent leadership problems are often problems of organizational structure, instead. Sometimes inappropriate people are, indeed, misplaced in leadership roles. But it is equally possible to design a leadership role for which it will be hard to find any appropriate person. The real problem may lie in the structure of the organization rather than in the characteristics of the people who head it.

Actually, many people seem to be effective leaders because they sense that leadership depends upon structure. Thus they ignore some leadership tasks and magnify others to make the position viable. Frequently a new man may improve a department which has long been in difficulty by emphasizing only some of the responsibilities of the department, neglecting others or shunting them off to some other division. It may be five years before anyone realizes that certain responsibilities are not being properly fulfilled or are creating strains for the other division, but meanwhile the successful leader has probably already moved beyond that job, leaving to an innocent successor a tangle of problems.

The Case of Headquarters Interference

The leadership-structure problem will be illustrated by examining a study by Robert Guest (25). He contrasts in vivid detail a poor plant leader and a good one who replaced him. A large assembly plant for an automobile company, Plant Y, had 5,000 employees. The poor leader, Mr. Stewart, did not solicit suggestions from his subordinates, bypassed his immediate subordinates, gave orders directly to those two or more levels below him, ruled by edict on the basis of fear rather than incentives, and carried out his threats by firing a number of people. His was a crisis-ridden operation; the only time people came together for meetings was in response to an emergency. Of the six plants in this division of the corporation, Plant Y had the poorest performance record, and it was getting worse.

Mr. Stewart was replaced by Mr. Cooley, who seemed to be a truly effective leader. Cooley mingled with the lower-level managers and foremen to obtain their cooperation and suggestions. At the outset he indicated that, although top management in the corporation thought deadwood should be removed from the staff, he disagreed and would give everyone ample opportunity to show his worth. (It developed, in fact, that only a handful of people in an organization of several thousand were dismissed during his regime.) He encouraged groups to meet regularly to solve common problems and, more important, to engage in long-range planning and consultation to prevent daily crises. He asked for and received money from headquarters to modernize the plant, starting first with the cafeteria and washrooms used by hourly employees. He brought staff-service representatives into contact with the line personnel. There they learned how irrelevant or self-defensive their services had been to the line. He inspired confidence and loyalty and erased the fear and crisis syndrome that had prevailed. After about six months, the plant started to improve its performance record, and within three years, it was the best of the six plants. Cooley was then transferred, and, even without him, the plant continued to perform very well.

Apparently, the big difference was style of leadership. Cooley was a good leader; Stewart wasn't. The corporation obviously thought so, for Stewart was given an early retirement when he was replaced, and Cooley was later promoted. But, Guest takes pains to point out in his sensitive analysis that leadership style was only one of two important factors. The other was that while Stewart received daily orders from division headquarters to correct specific situations, Cooley was left alone. Cooley was allowed to lead; Stewart was told how to lead.

Pieced together, the picture—which is far from complete—looks something like this. Stewart *was* a respected and competent manager. He was not new to the responsibility of running a large plant, and apparently the plant had performed adequately under his leadership until the end of the Korean War. At that time, in all six plants there was a rush to fill the demand for new automobiles whose production had been curtailed during the war. The speed of the lines was stepped up, two-shift operations were begun, new people were hired, and a large number of managers had to be placed in new jobs. All the plants were subject to strong stresses, but Plant Y had some of the oldest equipment and poorest layout in the division. Perhaps for this reason, Plant Y fell behind the others in its performance during the changeover from war-time to peace-time operations. The division managers had exerted immediate pressure and issued specific directives. They believed the problems were caused by Stewart's lack of control, rather than by equipment and layout factors. Managers in the plant commented that carrying out directives from division headquarters had become Stewart's chief preoccupation. Managers in such staff services as accounting, quality control, material control, and personnel also received specific directives from above. Thus, one of the cardinal rules of efficient bureaucracy appears to have been violated—managers were not allowed to manage within their sphere of competence. In effect, they were demoted; the shape of the authority structure changed from a pyramid with gradually sloping sides to one with sharply pitched sides, pushing authority up to company headquarters.

The headquarters had withdrawn legitimate authority from the plant manager and from the heads of staff departments. This left them no choice but to withdraw authority from the people under them, because division headquarters' orders described specific action involving the people reporting to the division manager and staff leaders. Thus, subordinates behaved in the same way as their superiors; that is, they complained that their legitimate authority had been withdrawn. Guest notes that at each level of management, officials reported that they were no longer allowed to run their own departments or stations, because someone from above either dictated decisions or gave orders directly to their subordinates. The more managers at all levels lost control of their own responsibilities and interfered in those of their subordinates, the less overall control there was and the more headquarters had to interfere, exaggerating the situation.

Cooley, the new manager, apparently sized up this situation accurately. He received assurances from the corporation headquarters that there would be no interference and that he was free to proceed in any manner he saw fit. He may even have been promised a fairly reasonable time period (say one year) for this freedom, but Guest gives no details. Contracting stopped, and managers once again were able to exercise the authority which should have been theirs. The formal structure was not changed. Though Guest at one point suggests that informal communications increased on a lateral basis, thus helping the formal structure to operate, there was nothing in the formal organization to prevent (or even to discourage) lateral communication. Lateral communication was demanded by the flow of work, and any barriers that had existed had been built up artificially through such practices as contracting. Meetings, once held only during crises, were now devoted to planning. Specific situations were corrected. For example, the work-standards department had usurped authority to describe the job content of certain individuals, rather than the standards of output of units.

What can we learn from Guest's data? As Guest says, Cooley probably could not have succeeded if the division had not let him alone; leadership was not enough. Therefore, the most important factor was the situation in which the two leaders, Cooley and Stewart, operated. Undoubtedly, the talents of each man played a role; that is, if Stewart had been asked to take over the plant under the same circumstances in which Cooley found it, one doubts that he would have had the same flair as Cooley, but one cannot be sure. Remarkably, many of Cooley's subordinates behaved as ideal leaders should. Yet, they were poor leaders under the old manager after the changeover to peace-time production.

One suspects, then, that for these people the situation was more important than any individual leadership traits or styles.

The same may have held true for Stewart; the stress of a rapid
changeover in an old plant, with top management giving him little
leeway, may have changed his leadership style. However, it is more
likely that Stewart would have been a good leader for a routine situation, but a poor one during such a crisis. So, leadership does play a role,
but not necessarily the most important one; it is better to begin, at least,
by examining the situation which the leader confronts.

Scientific Administration

I have been emphasizing the importance of a structural view of
organizations. What, then, is the value of the scientific-administration
approach, which considers crucial such matters as the span of control,
unity of command, the "scalar principle" (a clear hierarchy of authority), staff and line separation? It is fashionable in social science circles to
ridicule this venerable school of thought, which continues to pour out
its large quota of text books and served as the guide for organizing the
federal government through the Hoover Commission reports on governmental reorganization. In many respects scientific-management theorists
take a structural view of organizations, but in many respects one very
different from the one advocated here. To understand the significance of
this approach, it is necessary to understand how it was born and bred,
and what it looks like today.

Scientific management theory, associated with such names as
Frederick Taylor, Luther Gulick, Lyndall Urwick, James D. Mooney,
Henri Fayol, and others, came to fruition in the 1930s and 1940s.[1] It
was built on the experiences of governmental and especially economic
organizations in the first third of the century. It observed practices in
leading organizations, and attempted to rationalize and explain them, as
is true of all schools of organizational theory. It set forth general principles that appeared to be consistent with observed practices and then
promoted them with vigor. Scientific management has been severely
criticized as being simplistic, propounding contradictory "principles,"
and being "normative" rather than "empirical"—saying what ought to

[1] For a good review of this tradition see Massie (42).

be rather than looking at what is. But the force of these legitimate criticisms peters out when one realizes that, with the exception of Max Weber in Germany, these were the first efforts to analyze management practices and to try to generalize them; these men were dealing with a new animal which had just lumbered onto the industrial landscape and which promised to be an exceedingly large and complex beast indeed.

This new creature was the complex industrial and governmental organization. It was composed of large sub-units (e.g., plants or divisions) which had to be coordinated from above; it engaged in complex and interdependent tasks with a changing technology; and it developed and utilized specialists such as engineers, scientists, accountants, sales executives, and traffic-control men. Much of what we take for granted today was new in the first third of this century. Today, through TV, novels, and contact with colleges, universities, and governmental agencies, the typical student has a fair idea of what goes on in large organizations. But in the 1920s and 1930s, the principles being enunciated by the management school were less obvious. Indeed, many of them are still violated in organizations today. Scientific-management theorists prescribed a span of control of about five (the number of men reporting to a supervisor), but one finds 20 men reporting to a company president or the administrative head of an agency. They advocated unity of command, but we find units being given contradictory orders by two or three different groups above them. They developed the idea that managers should only deal with exceptions and planning, not with daily routines, but many organizations do not distinguish between routine administration and long-range policy formulation. These are only a few examples. Numerous management-consultant groups make a handsome living by pointing out the inefficiency of such practices, using the simple ideas of the management-science movement.

Nor have the ideas of that movement remained so simple. The school has gradually incorporated other perspectives, and, for greater flexibility, has also been developing more complex statements of principles. These ideas continue to be a major basis for organizational behavior, not only because of their successful propagation and establishment in countless business schools, but because they recommend themselves on the basis of "common sense." Since the principles are based on observation of actual organizations, it is not surprising that there is a congruity between the evolved trial-and-error practices of organizations and the principles of the theorists and consultants who studied them and wrote about them.

A recent issue of *Fortune* illustrates the durability of the scientific-administration school. While one article reviews the latest in human-relations techniques and describes their effectiveness, another explores the rapid and very profitable growth of the candy company, Mars, Inc., dominated by a man who passes out copies of Fayol and Urwick to his managers (46). But this school of thought is fighting a rear-guard action in the groves of academe if not in the stony field of actual organizations. The nature of organizations is changing, and more important, the research of social scientists and their value judgments has placed the scientific-management theorists on the defensive.

What was good for the Pennsylvania Railroad in the 1920s or the Bureau of the Budget and the Department of Agriculture in the 1930s just did not seem adequate to the challenges of the 1950s. The proportion of blue-collar workers in industry was declining at that time, and the proportion of white-collar workers, especially lower and middle management, was rising very rapidly. It also became harder to attract and retain professionals, such as engineers and scientists. White-collar technicians had to be treated differently from the men promoted from the ranks or the nephew of the owner. The technicians were more numerous, they had more mobility among organizations, and they were becoming more expensive. Similar problems appeared in nonprofit organizations. More professionals were being employed by the federal government and by state and local government agencies such as hospitals and community service departments. Furthermore, the tasks of the organizations were changing. Routine work was increasingly taken over by mechanical devices while management was more and more concerned with new markets and problems for which there were few precedents. The old-line salesmen in the sales department were replaced by sophisticated technicians in a marketing department. The uneducated guard in the prison was asked to take directions from a clinical psychologist. All organizations were required to plan ahead and to make or interpret forecasts. What had been a fairly easy solution—designating a few people as staff and the rest as line—increasingly came under criticism as the staff began to outnumber the line and nobody could tell the difference. The old simple model of an organization would not suffice.

Business and governmental organizations turned to whatever source of help they could get. Social scientists and business administration people were standing ready with a wide range of solutions, usually based upon the experimentation of a few pioneering firms. But for most organizations the search for new methods was the result of the influence of semipopular magazines such as the *Harvard Business Review* or the *Public Administration Review*, associations like the American Management Association or its counterparts in governmental and voluntary organizational circles, and the growing and aggressive management-consulting industry.

An attempt to date the beginning of the new management movement can go far back into history. In his fascinating discussion of changes in organizational ideology in the military, Morris Janowitz notes that a prize-winning essay on leadership and discipline published in a military journal in 1905 marks the beginning of an attempt to shift from sheer authoritarianism to more rational principles of management of military men. Manipulation, persuasion, and group consensus were stressed at that time by none other than an infantry officer (30, p.38). Even the scientific-management movement was stressing cooperation between employees and employers in the first decade of the century, though the terms were somewhat different from present statements. Reinhard Bendix (2, ch. 5) traces in detail the adjustment of "managerial ideologies"—their justification for commanding—in U.S. industry to changes in the social and technological environment.

But it was the writing of Elton Mayo and Chester Barnard and others in the 1930s which raised the standard of what came to be called, very loosely, the "human-relations movement" in industry. Again, as in the case of scientific-management techniques, adoption of human-relations techniques by any sizeable number of organizations lagged a decade or two behind the ideological codifications in published books. Partly influenced by this movement, and partly as a result of the changing nature of organizations and increased sophistication, the frontal attacks on scientific management came in the late 1940s. In 1947 Herbert Simon, a political scientist, published his enormously influential *Administrative Behavior*. This was a wholesale attack on the principles of the scientific-management school and an acceptance of the leading tenets of the human-relations movement (75). The very title is indicative; the emphasis is upon administrators, rather than managers (presumably a broader term and a less authoritarian one), and upon behavior, rather than principles. The next year another political scientist, Dwight Waldo, published another and even more scathing attack, this time directed towards public institutions, called *The Administrative State* (86). The folly of the simplistic notions and confident principles of scientific management was exposed—at least as far as academicians were concerned. However, whether the work of Mayo, Barnard, Simon, and Waldo was a practical substitute for the sure guidance of the management theorists and consultants was another question. Vague generalities and implicit principles and normative bias are evident in the work of these scholars.

But our concern here is with a cool critique of scientific management, rather than with the wave of abuse that swept over it. The major criticism of these theorists may not be that they had a mechanistic view of man; they often admitted the importance of informal social relations and noneconomic motives. More important, they insisted that an organization cannot be designed on the basis of the kinds of informal relations that grow up in an organization. Rather, they held that the design must minimize the opportunity for unfortunate and uncontrollable informal relations, leaving room only for the necessary ones. Their view of man was simplistic, but in laying out general principles and designing structures, their simple views were probably adequate to the task. More complex views were a luxury neither they nor the organizations they addressed themselves to could well afford when so little else was known. (Such indulgence is now possible.) Their principles were often contradictory. Still, no one has yet replaced their principles concerning, for example, whether to organize by purpose, place, or clientele. If their search for the optimum span of control for executives (the number of men one man could supervise) was idealistic, no better bases for organizing authority were presented by their critics. We now know, from empirical studies, that span of control can effectively vary from one to 20 or more; it depends upon the kind of task that must be carried out.[2] But that obvious and important point was not made by the critics of scientific management. To find the true deficiencies of the scientific-management approach, one must step back a little and examine the basic flaw in most approaches—their attempt to enunciate principles, laws, hypotheses, theorems, postulates (or whatever the current terminology) which apply to *all* organizations, rather than to *specific* types of organizations.

A General Theory versus Specific Theories

Can there be one theory of *organization* or should there be many *theories* of organizations? This is the basic issue which confronts the practical theorist. The scientific-management school is not unique in

<hr />

[2] See the discussion of this issue in Perrow (59).

propounding concepts which supposedly will apply to all organizations. This is the aim of most sociologists, as well as of psychologists, social psychologists, and economists. The natural-science model demands that our theories be generally applicable. This rigidity has performed a disservice to organizational theory. It has prevented us from recognizing that there are various types of organizations and thus that we may legitimately have theories that only apply to some types and not to others. We know enough about organizations now to recognize that most generalizations that are applicable to all organizations are too obvious, or too general, to be of much use for specific predictions. This was not true in the past when there was less organizational knowledge, fewer complex organizations, and fewer organizational varieties. One of the dominant themes of this book will be that today organizations come in great variety and that organizational theory must be varied to be useful.

For example, under which circumstances can a span of control of 15 be effective, and when should control be limited to two or three? The scientific-management school maintains that too large or too small spans are always harmful. However, we now know enough to suggest that a large span of control is effective when subordinates are performing routine similar tasks which involve a minimum of interdependence, discretion, uncertainty. In such circumstances one man can effectively supervise all. But if the tasks are not routine, if they require discretion and if there is considerable interdependence and uncertainty surrounding them, the span of control is best kept small. This permits the subordinates and their superior to consult frequently, to exchange information and ideas, and frequently to reshuffle responsibilities in the search for optimal solutions to difficult problems. Indeed, since such subordinates have a good deal of discretion, they are likely to have specialized skills and considerable training; thus, they would resist the "mechanistic" control of routine reports and scheduled reviews which might be effective in a more routine situation. In contrast, subordinates in routine situations, who have few skills, are likely to prefer highly structured controls.

To take another instance, when should "lateral" or "diagonal" communication occur (communication across department lines rather than vertically within departments)? The human-relations school would argue that lateral communication is useful in all situations; the scientific-management school argues that communication should be vertical, in order to keep lines of authority and responsibility clear. For example, Wilfred Brown, an able British manager, argues in his *Explorations in*

Management (9) that communications and decision-making should be made at the "crossover" point between two units—the point at which one man has authority over both units—rather than below it. Otherwise, people without sufficient grasp of the total situation and awareness of all the implications will be making decisions or will communicate incomplete and possibly misleading information. But others argue this involves delay and a heavy load on communication lines, and those below the crossover point may really be more informed about the matter than their common superior. Besides, initiative and enlarged authority should be fostered at lower levels.

Once again, the solution seems to lie in the nature of the work performed by the organization or in the ability of the structure of the organization to incorporate change rapidly. Lateral communication and decision making below the crossover points are potentially dangerous in routine situations where there are standard instructions (programs) for work and well-specified decision points. In such circumstances, irrelevant stimuli, such as bits of information, must be eliminated; the basis for deciding what must be communicated should be simplified. But in situations where it is difficult to devise standardized instructions and decisions must be made by people close to the operation, regardless of their rank, lateral communication is essential. If it is absent, there is danger to coordination of units which cannot be completely controlled from the crossover point.

It is apparent, then, that both the scientific-management school and the human-relations school have useful ideas to contribute, but they apply to different situations. Sophisticated advocates in each camp would admit to "exceptions" where their approach might not work. However, the virtue of the structural viewpoint is that it attempts to use such exceptions as a basis for rules, by diagnosing the particular characteristics of such situations rather than adhering to the "one-best" way.

The Socio-Technical School

One other approach to organizational analysis deserves a brief comment. In England human-relations techniques have been wedded, somewhat oddly, to a technical view of organizations, resulting in what is called the socio-technical approach.[3] According to this perspective, the social relations that develop in a work place are related to the techno-

---

[3] See, for example, Rice (61).

logical character of the work—such as the kind of interaction the job allows, the degree of cooperation required, and the possibility or impossibility of measuring individual effort in a joint task. Changing the technology is likely to result in change in social relations. In the United States this view has been fruitfully employed in studies of assembly-line workers and of automated production systems. Because this approach at least implicitly removed the human-relations perspective from the void of universalistic principles, it has proved stimulating and valuable. Endless debates about the role of the foreman are obviated when it becomes clear that his function varies with the technical work system. In some cases, he manages men and impels them to their maximum effort. In other cases, he is a servant to the production workers, supplying them with tools, material, information, and help in technical problems.

However, the work of socio-technical systems groups has been generally confined to the supervisor-operative level. Until recently it has not been generalized to larger organizational units. But the breakthrough was important, because it provided a systematic basis for noting differences among organizations.

It should be noted that there are other perspectives concerning organizations which will not be discussed here. Some are small, specialized offshoots of those already mentioned. Others are not really guides to the study of organizations but are used for other purposes. For example, much microeconomic theory, while it certainly relates to the organization of productive units, is not concerned in any significant detail with organizations *per se*. For microeconomic theory, it is sufficient to consider the firm as an undifferentiated unit (often the shadow of one man); only limited assumptions about its characteristics are needed. Other theories which fall under the organizational rubric merely use organizations as a setting for studying human behavior. Much psychological and social-psychological work falls in this category; this includes a good deal of the theory concerning decision making or group dynamics. With these we are only marginally concerned because our unit of analysis is the organization as a whole or some large subsystem of the organization rather than human behavior in groups.

The Sociological Perspective and Its Limitations

The psychologist deals primarily with individuals, the social psychologist with small groups, and the sociologist with large groups or aggregates (organizations, social classes) and their patterned relationships. However, the distinction between these disciplines does not rest on the size of the groups they study. The sociologist, for example, is less concerned with the distinctive qualities of individuals than with the qualities of classes of individuals—such as lower-class families, religious organizations, Negroes in urban slums. He examines their norms and values, their relationships with other groups, and their patterns of behavior, to which he often refers as their structure. He often deals with the "central tendencies" of groups or aggregates of people. Thus, not all members of fraternities on a campus have wealthy parents, but there will be proportionally more sons of such parents among fraternity members than among those not belonging to fraternities. He may, however, examine the nature of the exceptional cases—e.g., he might find, as one study did, that those students who came from lower-class backgrounds and joined fraternities were more likely to indicate that they were "not very close" to their parents than middle-class students in fraternities, and not as close to their parents as lower-class students not in fraternities.

When the sociologist turns to formal organizations he again emphasizes central tendencies of groups. While recognizing that one person, say a powerful executive, can have a profound impact upon an organization, he is more likely to ask such questions as what kind of organizations (in terms of such criteria as size, stages of growth, environmental pressures) are likely to have powerful executives and what kinds are likely to have less powerful ones? Or, what kind of group relations within an organization are likely to generate a demand for powerful executives?

The sociologist makes only minimal and quite crude assumptions about the psychology of individuals. (To psychologists they will certainly seem crude.) He tends to make rather crude assumptions about the interactions of people, too (at least from the standpoint of the social psychologist), because it is the goal of his professional discipline to study the patterned regularities of interaction among groups, or social structure. For instance, that sales and production tend to be in conflict in economic organizations is not due to the propensity to quarrel among people who happen to get jobs in sales and production, but rather due to the differing ends or values of these two groups. Thus simply stated, the conclusion becomes obvious. Nevertheless, much organizational analysis explores individual psychology in order to explain organizational behavior. In contrast, the sociologist is interested in tracing the implications of group differences. Why do they exist? Under what circumstances is the conflict between sales and production great and when is it small? What are the "mechanisms" for handling this conflict? Should or can the conflict be reduced, or should it only be "managed"? Would sales re-organization help? Would a change in the market situation have an effect? All these findings are unrelated to the psychological character-istics of individuals or to the interaction of specific individuals. Of course, in the interactions of the vice-president of sales and the vice-president of production we have social-psychological aspects, but the sociologist prefers to consider these two individuals as people filling roles which are tied to the patterned regularities within their respective groups. Thus, he minimizes the social-psychological aspects and maxi-mizes the structural aspect.

While the sociologist adopts a cruder concept of human nature than the psychologist, his approach is probably more sophisticated than that of the economist. Though economic interpretations of behavior are found in sociology, the sociologist is more likely to avoid the stereotype of the economic man. He views organizations as having multiple and conflicting goals rather than single goals, as most economists see them. This is no criticism of economists. Their approach is inherent in the nature of the problems with which they deal and the data they utilize.

The sociologist's concern with norms and values is inevitably re-flected in his writings. Sociologists aim to be "value-free" in their analyses—objective, dispassionate, neutral. However, the student should recognize the occupational hazards of this work and discount those conclusions which appear to be "normatively biased"—as the jargon has it. The conclusions may indeed be objectively correct, but it is legitimate to be suspicious of them. The economist is in a much better position in this respect. He works with data several times removed from ongoing situations which involve the behavior of the individuals. The data of the sociologist, however, are much more immediate, emotionally laden, subject to perceptual biases not only of the sociologist himself but also of the individual who is the source of information. More important, the sociologist can hardly help becoming identified with the organization he is studying or with some of its aspects, and thus he may take sides. It is easier for the economist to be detached about the level of investment of all manufacturing firms than for the sociologist to remain detached from the squabbles, infighting, and "obvious inefficiencies" of a particular organization. When the study involves not individual organizations (case studies) but an analysis of many organizations, in which it is possible to use more "objective" data—such as size, technology, turnover rates, and skill ratios—objectivity is easier. Nevertheless, the sociologist must still spend a good deal of time in the muddy fields of particular groups and first-hand observations. It is well for the student to bear this situation in mind.

The greatest problem for the sociologist (and the social psychologist) is predicting behavior on the basis of studies of attitudes or studies of artificial group situations. Interviews or questionnaires are frequently a major means of determining how people feel about various subjects; then we assume their behavior will be consistent with the attitudes they expressed. But the questions may be poor, resulting in misleading answers. More important, past experience with human behavior indicates that attitudes are not necessarily good guarantees of subsequent behavior. What people actually do is influenced not only by their attitudes but also by the specific situations in which they find themselves. To confound the matter further, the student's tendency is to rely upon aggregations of attitudes. If we find that 80 percent of the supervisors in a state welfare agency give responses to a questionnaire indicating that they would put organizational stability ahead of client service, not only do we not know if these respondents would *really* attempt this, but we also do not know if they have the power to do so. Perhaps if some of the remaining 20 percent attempt to tip organizational practices in favor of client services the other will behave the same way. We can observe the organization over a long period of time, of course, and devise various "objective" measures regarding stability and service. But this is expensive and time-consuming. Moreover, the results would not really show whether the preferences of the officials had much to do with the behavior of the organization. Perhaps the nature of the clients had shifted; or perhaps the legislature had increased the budget sufficiently to make both goals possible; or possibly the political situation in the state was the decisive factor.

Nor can we be certain that carefully controlled experiments in small-group laboratories have much relationship to behavior in the outside world. It has been found that, try as one might, the biases of the researchers affect the outcome (64). Furthermore, the subjects of experiments presumably behave differently in highly temporary situations than in enduring ones. In situations where they do not care too much what the other subjects think of them, their behavior is different from the way it is when they are observed by their friends and co-workers.

One of the best illustrations of the relationship between attitudes and behavior may be found in an ingenious study made some 30 years ago. A Chinese couple and a Caucasian travelled throughout the United States, stopping at a representative sample of motels and hotels, seeking accommodations. Of the 251 establishments visited, only one *refused* to accommodate them. Six months later questionnaires were sent to these establishments as well as to others in the area asking if they would give accommodations to a Chinese couple. Fully 91 percent said they would *not*.[4] Obviously, questionnaire reports of behavior were at odds with actual behavior; the measure of the "values" of these proprietors proved to be a very poor predictor of the way they actually behaved.

Fortunately, in most organizational studies questionnaires are combined with observations and records, thus yielding some check upon the reliability of the questionnaire data. Ideally, observations of behavior over an extended period of time are used as the basis for drawing up questionnaires which will provide data which could be replicated by anyone else. If the researcher publishes his questions and findings, presumably somebody else could take the same questions, survey the same organizations or a similar organization, and receive the same responses. Such a retest should provide an objective test of the observations. Unfortunately, however, there have been few replications of studies in the sociology of organizations. Most students are too eager to generate new ideas and "prove" their own hypotheses to go through the routine and somehow subservient task of checking somebody else's findings.

Nevertheless, with all of these limitations (the other social sciences share some and have additional grave ones of their own) the sociological approach to organizational analysis offers distinctive advantages. For some kinds of problems it is superior to other approaches, even though for other problems it is inferior and has little to say. The structure and group relations of a hospital will have far less to do with its effectiveness than medical innovations in antibiotics, but the sociologist can predict with some authority which hospitals are likely to utilize new drugs first. The timing and rapidity of the revolutionary changes that occurred in the Department of Defense in the 1960s could not have been predicted by a sociologist. In that case, one man, Defense Secretary Robert

[4] This study is reported in a challenging and provocative article on this general subject by Deutscher (16, p. 249).

McNamara, changed a hidebound institution. However, once those changes were undertaken, sociologists could readily have predicted their extension to other units of government and their impact upon private industry and upon the defensive strategies of groups within the Defense Department.

chapter
two
The Variety
of the Species

In Chapter One I argued that a social-structural view of organizations has much to recommend it, at least as a starting point in organizational analysis. One other advantage of this approach, thus far touched upon only lightly, will be explored in this chapter. The structural view of organizations provides the most convenient tool for analyzing differences among organizations. Organizational theory, no matter which variety is utilized, is sophisticated enough at the present time to deal with the basic aspects of all organizations. We know, for example, that some form of leadership is necessary in all organizations, that some form of structure of communications and controls is necessary, that there must be a technology to transform an organization's raw materials. The student is likely to fall asleep over enunciations of the general principles that apply to all organizations. What is needed is some way to deal with differences among organizations. Whether you are going to work in an organization or plan to do research concerning it, you must know what makes it distinctive.

The view that "organizations are, after all, made up of human beings" is not likely to reveal much about the distinctive character of organizations. In one of the strongest statements of the social-psychological viewpoint, the first half of the highly respected volume by James March and Herbert Simon, *Organizations* (41), 160 or so propositions are stated in the course of four chapters without any indication that these truths might apply to some types of organizations but not to others. From this point of view, all organizations are basically similar. The same attitude is generally held in the management-science view of organizations.

The leadership view of organizations has begun to make some discriminations among types of organizations but one of the leading theorists in this field, Renesis Likert, concludes by presenting prescriptions for all organizations. A curious middle chapter in his book (Chapter 6, *New Patterns of Management* (37)) toys with the idea that there are perhaps two types of organizations: those which deal with repetitive events and those which do not. But in the rest of the book, dealing with prescriptions for good management, the implications of this distinction are followed no further.

In contrast, the structural view has a ready-made tool for distinguishing organizations. Since this approach focuses upon structures, it must deal with the whole rather than with parts or particular processes; it is forced to ask how structures differ. Are they centralized or decentralized? Are there many autonomous parts or only a few? The structural view is less likely to lead to statements that there is one best way of designing or running an organization; those who use the approach observe and record the variety of forms that exist.

Most criteria used for contrasting different types of organizations are related to the organizations' manifest function for society or the manner in which they are controlled. That is, we commonly distinguish schools from factories or public institutions from private institutions. As obvious as these distinctions are, they tell us relatively little about the structure of an organization. Some schools are run like factories, some factories have the atmosphere of experimental schools. Whether or not an organization is producing a profit or operating at the lowest possible cost is another faulty divining rod for determining how organizations differ.

Two Correctional Institutions

What follows is a description, taken from a published study, of two living units (cottages) in two juvenile correctional institutions. This material, plus additional information about the two institutions, will provide the basis for a discussion of how to conceptualize the differences between the organizations—that is, what kinds of intellectual tools or concepts are useful for discriminating between them. This investigation will provide some building blocks for considering the variety of organizational forms which do exist. Next a similar inquiry will be made concerning two business organizations. As you read the following description, ask yourself how you would describe, in terms of concepts rather than of behavior, the difference between the two institutions (78, pp. 155–158). (In both living units, the youths were about 14 to 16 years old.)

That there were sharp contrasts in the rounds of life between institutions is shown emphatically in the following quotations—lengthy but worthwhile—from the field notes of observers who viewed the early evening activities in cottages at Dick and Inland. The observer at Dick wrote:

When boys leave the playing field, the commander [supervisor] just gives a signal to the outline boys [boys who help in supervision] and they shape them up. They call them in and get them lined up, the boys stretch out their arms so they can be counted, and then they walk over to the building. They stand outside the door until the commander gets there, he looks them over and nods to the outline boys, and the outline boys then take the kids in and upstairs. They march up a ramp—up three floors to the top floor . . . [to] a huge long room with no partitions, in the middle of which sits a platform on which there is a chair where the commander can watch the boys at all times. The commander depended pretty much on the outline boys to keep order. Individual boys would come over to him raising their hands asking, "Please sir, may I go to the bathroom" or something like that, and he would nod and the boy would go off.

The boys filed into the room and broke up into two groups . . . both lined up until the commander gave the signal to dismiss. One group stayed there, took off their clothes, laid them on the bench, then lined up again along the bench naked and stood at attention until they were all ready. Then the outline boy gave them a signal and they marched into the shower room. The showers had already been turned on by K, one of the outline boys. They took a shower and then turned off the water and stood there till K told them to move on to the other side of the room; still in line, they filed past him or another outline boy and were handed small towels one by one. They dried themselves, hung their towels on a rack at the end of the shower room, made another formation, and stood in line till K gave them the word to come out. They marched out and back around the benches again and got their clothes.

Meanwhile, another group had lined up and the same procedure was followed. . . . One outline boy stood at the door of the bathroom to watch anything that went on in the bathroom. There was very little noise in the place, very little talking. [The commander] said that after they had gotten all cleaned up, etc., that he would allow them to sit around the tables and talk, play card games, or something like that, as long as they talked in low voices; then later on they would go to their bunks and watch television. . . . [The commander] told us that he had three boys who needed to be punished. They had been talking in the dining hall. He called out their names. The boys came up, stood at the platform, held on with their hands and bent over, and the commander took a paddle that was about a yard long and struck each of them three very hefty blows. All of the boys in the place stopped and watched rather sullenly, and I kind of flinched with each blow. The boy who was being punished, however, kept absolutely quiet and firm, and when the blow was over, he walked off as dignified as he could. . . . The commander in all this was a Mr. X., who . . . says you can't let the boys out of sight; the boys can't be trusted. You have to punish them . . . some of them have never been punished before and they have told him that.

Very different is this report from Inland:

We went to dinner soon, where the boys were unusually restless. First they griped about the leftovers from Sunday, chicken and roast beef, and then they started to jump up and run around trying to get something they wanted. Joe Walton, the counselor, warned them about this, but some of them kept it up, so he told Paterson, Sawkins, and Kearns that they had lost their treats. . . . Paterson got real sore, blew up, and kept this up for quite a while. So did Kearns, but he didn't make it last so long. After supper I went back to Middle Cottage and wandered into Room No. 5, which is occupied by Dan Sawkins and Frank Dickson. Sawkins was playing records, of which he has quite a collection. Different boys wandered in and stayed for a while to listen. Greg Wilkins stayed the longest. . . . He and a couple of the others did a little solo dance now and then. . . . Barry Wink came in for a while too. He and Sawkins seemed to like each other pretty much. . . . Owen Dukes wandered in and out, usually doing a kind of solo dance and doing pretty well, too. First Sawkins, and then a few of the others, would light up a cigarette in their room. This is against the rules on the second floor, but they showed by this that they trusted me and didn't mind my seeing what they did. . . .

After listening to about a dozen records, O'Bannon asked me if I wanted to play poker or rummy, and he got ahold of Dukes and Sawkins and they said they would, too. We went down to the first floor to the rec room. . . . Sawkins and I lost the pinochle game we were in, so another pair sat in instead of us. Then Jack Corbett wanted to play rummy in his room. So I went in and played two-hand rummy with him. He said he liked to be alone from the noise of the other rooms. . . . While we were playing, a number of fellows came in off and on to ask for cigarettes, and usually he said O.K. Greg Wilkins came in too and sat on the floor reading one of Corbett's comic books. A boy from another cottage came to the window to get a suitcase from Corbett through the window. Evidently there's something wrong with giving or trading things to others on loan, because they didn't do it through the usual passage-way. The staff members in Middle Cottage seem to regard Corbett as a pain in the neck because he seldom does what he is told to do. Actually, he does a lot of smoking on the second floor and even in the staff room itself, in spite of what they say to him; and he feels he doesn't have much to worry about because he doesn't care much if he goes home or not. That seems to be the worst thing they can do to him—to take away a vacation leave. But once in a while they remind him that he could be sent back to court [which might send him to a harsher institution]. He's sure they wouldn't do that for the little things he's been doing, but it's the continual little things that get them down.

Before we finished the rummy game, Joe Walker came by and wanted me to play pinochle, so I went down shortly. . . . Before we finished this pinochle game, it was time for cleanup, as Walton [a counselor] called out; and Paterson was the one who was organizing it this time. . . . Paterson had already blown up tonight, so I was surprised to see him getting things going. We stopped our card game in the middle of a hand to get going on the cleanup. Little Phil Daniels made an announcement while the treat was being passed out . . . that they were starting a new paper and that there was to be a big prize of a 25 cent candy bar to each boy in the cottage, whichever cottage came up with the best name for it.

By 9:30 they were almost ready to start to bed. Tonight Joe Walton was pretty worn out after an hour or two of trying to get them to go to bed. They would be in and out, start horsing around, come into the hall, talk to somebody in another room, play their radio too loud, their record player too loud. . . . Joe Walker got peeved at the two boys in his room and came out in the hall and sat on the floor until everything had quieted down, about an hour later. Since Brownell has moved, Owen Dukes is alone in his room. He has a morbid fear of the dark, so little Daniels went in with him to keep him company for the night. All of the boys are very friendly toward me now. They come up to me with their favorite stories, and they all said good night. . . . [All names are pseudonyms.][1]

Some more general remarks can be made about these two institutions. At Dick, the first one, punishments were severe. There was an isolation cell, commonly called the dungeon, where runaways were incarcerated for two or three days, subsisted on a diet of milk and bread, slept on a bench, with a blanket in the winter, and used a can for sanitary purposes. There were no windows in the cell; it was dark and airless. Mute testimony to the rage and enforced idleness of the occupants was provided when the superintendent of the institution proudly pointed out how they were able to claw away bits of brick and mortar at the top of the cell where there was a small slit for light and air. He remarked that one would hardly believe that one could do this with one's bare hands especially since one had to hang from the ledge while doing it. Runaways were also punished by having their heads shaved and being forced to sit on a bench for several days during activities. They were paddled an estimated 30 to 40 strokes.

The structure of the institution was quite centralized. In theory, the commanders of the various cottages were free to run their units as they wished as long as there were no escapes, or the boys did not get out of line in the dining hall, or did not straggle when moving from the school building to their cottage. But despite the autonomy of the

---

[1] Reprinted by permission of The Macmillan Company from *Organization for Treatment*, by David Street, Robert Vinter, and Charles Perrow. Copyright © by The Free Press, a division of The Macmillan Company, in 1966.

commanders, variations in practice were few since it was generally accepted that the only way to maintain order and inculcate discipline and respect in the boys was through rigid programming and insistence upon obedience. Typical variations were minor: one commander allowed whispering at meal time as long as it was quiet and only intermittent; at the same time, another commander insisted upon absolute silence, even to the extent of using sign language for passing salt and pepper. All cottage commanders answered directly to the administrator of the institution, and there was a minimal degree of departmentalization or specialization. One man, a former used-car salesman, was designated as social-service director. The administrator said he wouldn't hire a trained social worker because they don't know how to punish. Only in the school was professional training required. Schooling, however, was not taken too seriously; the production needs of the farm took precedence over education at various times of the year.

In marked contrast, the second institution, Inland, had a large staff of specialists trained in psychology or social work. In its rather decentralized system, most of the power resided in the clinical director of the institution, who gave considerable latitude to cottage parents and others in their choice of methods for handling boys (though there was a continuing program for educating and indoctrinating such personnel). The institution had very few sanctions for truancy or misbehavior and even then did not always apply them. For example, it was considered a healthy thing when several boys "ran away" from the institution one day. They simply gathered in a group and walked off the grounds and down a railroad track, then were picked up a couple of hours later and brought back in a station wagon. Their objective was to protest certain practices in some of the cottages, and their act was treated as such. They were not punished. Their protest, incidentally, concerned what they regarded as the disorderly way things were run.

What can be said about these two quite different organizations in the same line of business? It would tell us very little about organizations to observe (even if it were true) that one was run by a punitive or even ignorant administrator and the other by a sensitive, democratic administrator with a Ph.D. If the difference were simply a matter of the personality of the executive, it would still be necessary to argue that it was no accident that these personality types were in charge. In view of the behavior of other personnel and the structural differences, it seems unlikely that changing the executives would make a great deal of difference. Nor would it explain much to point to the dissimilar attitudes of the personnel in these two institutions. It may be recalled that in the first chapter it was suggested that, in another correctional institution, the impact of the institution upon attitudes of personnel was more important than the impact of the attitudes of personnel on the institution.

The main difference between these two institutions appears to be the conception of the nature of the "raw material" with which they dealt—the delinquents—and thus what was necessary to transform this raw material. Once a definition is embedded in a program, the opinions of personnel who remain at the institution become congruent with it. The staff at Dick tended to define delinquents as lacking in proper respect for parents and other adults, as not being trained to be obedient, as not to be trusted as much as other children, and as being almost a different breed of animal. Thus, to change these delinquents into law-abiding citizens it was necessary to teach them to be obedient, to have proper respect for adults, and to be trustworthy. Given such a goal, the means become clear. One should march these children about, discipline them severely, watch them every minute, and teach them to say "yes sir" and "no sir." In order to do this a tight, authoritarian organizational structure is necessary, and the staff must develop a firm, no-nonsense, hardnosed attitude. If the method is not successful—that is, if the children continue to get into trouble after they leave—that merely reinforces the ideology by indicating how bad is the material one has to work with. In terms of this view of the institution's task, the administrator was neither punitive nor ignorant. He stressed love and kindness *when the children deserved it*. The trouble was that in this environment the inmates rarely had much opportunity to show that they deserved affection. Besides, the pressures upon the staff to keep order were greater than the pressure to reward the deserving with love and kindness. The executive and his staff were truly committed to the job of rehabilitating delinquents, and they could not understand why some people might be appalled by their methods. For the type of task it had created for itself this was a viable institution, well-run and well-supervised; it met its goals as well as most organizations do.

Inland's concept of the nature of a delinquent was quite different. He was someone who had been let down by adults rather than one who had been coddled by adults. His problems were psychological and learning obedience had nothing to do with them. The psychologists and social workers probed into his past, his complexes, his attitudes toward authority and toward parents. They tried to get him to bring up "painful material." In fact, they often subtly encouraged some of the children to "act out" and create disturbances in the institution so that they might have a means of "getting to" the delinquent. They did not believe that delinquents were basically different from other people or necessarily untrustworthy, or even necessarily lacking in self-discipline. They thought that through sympathy, understanding, empathy, and a permissive environment the delinquent's personality could be changed. For this they needed an open structure, few rules, a decentralized institution, and patience and tolerance.

Both these organizations had the same "product"—rehabilitated delinquents—yet in some respects Dick resembled the way a factory is run, while Inland resembled the way a research and development firm might be run. Dick was trying to turn out a uniform product, felt that it knew exactly what was wrong with the raw material it received and how to change it, enjoyed complete agreement on the kinds of techniques that should be used, and generally processed the youngsters in a uniform matter. It did not need a large staff because significant economies could be practiced as long as the raw material was seen as basically similar. The staff did not need special training since their tasks were not very complex; anybody who had achieved adulthood and stayed out of prison could be expected to possess the necessary skills. In fact, Dick was staffed through a patronage system; whenever a new political party gained control of the state government there was a change of personnel, including the administrator (except teachers, who had some civil-service protection). Since few skills were required it mattered little that such a large turnover might occur every few years; similarly, the cost of hourly turnover in assembly-line factories is low. As in most routine organizations, the performance of any one individual was measured by minimum rather than by the maximum standards. As on an assembly line, there was little advantage in trying to increase the productivity at Dick (e.g., greater deference toward staff, greater speed in eating or marching to school). There were no rewards for speedups; indeed, they might jam the sequence of tightly scheduled activities.

In contrast, at Inland every youngster was considered unique. There was no one way of treating all of them. Each one required a great deal of examination and research. While standard procedures were necessary to run so complex an organization, every effort was made to provide individual programs and activities for the children. Staff members were carefully screened when they were hired and everything was done to retain them because it took some time to learn how to work effectively with such materials. Furthermore, some were more effective than others and could be rewarded for their success. Since the major performance criterion was changing attitudes, high productivity on the part of one man did not interfere with the work of others.

The point of the preceding descriptions and analysis is not to prove that some institutions are like factories, but to show that within the same "type" or organization—in this case a "people-changing institution"—a wide variety of techniques, structures, and goals can be used. In order to understand these differences it is important to find out how an organization conceives its task and its raw material, how interdependent is its system, how closely controlled it must be. What would work for one organization might not work for another, unless both had similar definitions of their raw material and similar techniques for transforming it. Nor would a training program to change the attitudes of the staff towards the raw material be very successful without a change in structure and techniques. Organizations comprise not only people but also techniques and structures. In fact, techniques and structures should be changed first because they are easier to change than established definitions of the raw material.

Only routine management skills would be required to improve the functioning of Dick while still keeping within the perspective in which it operated. A better layout of the work and sequence of activities might be devised; the school might be shut down entirely during the harvest and planting seasons, but run on an eight-hour day during the winter and summer. Or the large dining halls could be subdivided, to permit more careful surveillance and to reduce noise. They could provide more "treats" (they had ice cream once a week) or sports (they had a good boxing team and a drum-and-bugle corps—both consistent with their image of the children); for punishment, these privileges could be withdrawn to eliminate more extreme forms of discipline.

To improve the functioning of Inland, within its perspective, routine management skills would not be appropriate. What Inland required were ways to utilize the dynamics of group interaction more creatively, rather than to rely so heavily upon individual psychotherapy. Methods might be found to achieve better relations with the county juvenile court, which sent them many of their inmates. These were more difficult problems, not amenable to routine analysis and prescription. Of course, to transform Dick into an Inland-type of institution, or Inland into a Dick-type of institution (some groups in both states tried to make such changes), a massive restructuring and reeducation program would be needed.

Quite different recommendations and management techniques are appropriate in these two different situations. As obvious as this seems, nevertheless many business and government consulting services come equipped with neat packages of nostrums. Not surprisingly they find that every organization they advise needs just what is in their package, whether it be a better data-processing system, linear programming, human-relations programs or executive-development programs, better control techniques, or a better marketing system.

Two Industrial Firms

In the economic area examples of organizational contrast may be drawn from studies made by Tom Burns and G. M. Stalker in *The Management of Innovation* (10). The first firm they described in some detail is a rayon mill in England. The technical details are not important in themselves but are necessary for getting a sense of the work flow of this type of organization. In the case of the second firm it is not clear just what they make beyond electronic components, but the information is probably less essential. Note the highly stable, highly structured, bureaucratic character of the firm described in the first extract:

> It is convenient at this point to go outside engineering and describe the working of a concern in a process industry, the subject of the first preliminary study. The plant produced viscose rayon filament yarn, and employed about 900 persons. It was owned by a company with offices in London and one smaller factory in Lancashire. Sales and costing were operated by the London office, but all other departments of the firm were represented in the factory.
>
> The production process proper starts with the intake of raw material into the stores. The principal materials are cellulose, carbon bisulphide, and sulphuric acid. The first stage is the arrangement of the stored cellulose sheets into batches of uniform weight. One man and a girl do this, with no mechanical aids apart from a weighing machine and a hand trolley. Although this stage can be referred to as a single interpretative step in the series, it obviously can be broken down into a large number of detailed movements; the essential point for us is that each separate movement is almost literally a "translation," even to the transport of a batch from the platform of the weighing machine to the place by the end door where its arrival denotes its readiness

for the next stage. This involves handcarting to a vat of caustic solution in which the batch is steeped for a period; at the end of this time, the cellulose is pressed between plates by a hydraulic ram, then carted and fed in to mechanical kneaders. The shredded cellulose is then stored for two or three days in mercerizing rooms in order to ensure a completely homogeneous moisture content and to prepare for the next chemical process, which is mixing with carbon bisulphide in mechanical churns. After this, the product, cellulose xanthate, is dropped through chutes into mixers, in which the compound is dissolved in a solution of caustic soda and mixed by beating and forcing through blend jackets into a homogeneous fluid. The viscose is stored under vacuum to remove bubbles, filtered, and then stored again in charge tanks.

All the stages up to this are preparatory. The next stage is central to the whole process. It consists in pumping the viscose through a multiple jet into a bath of sulphuric acid, from which it emerges as solid fibres. These are drawn up over a wheel, twisted to form a thread, and passed down into a spinning pot, in which the thread is built up into cylindrical cakes. The finishing processes consist of washing the cake with neutralizing solutions and water, drying it in heated lockers, inspecting, and so on to weighing and dispatch.

So far we have included in the system no more than certain muscular and mechanical efforts and chemical processes. At the same technical level there are a number of actions which are not themselves part of the processes of change, as we have so far noted them, but are essential to their proper performance. The spinning machine, for example, is automatic, but a number of workers are present renewing broken threads, removing completed cakes, and replacing empty pots, an operation which involves stopping and starting the machine. In the mercerizing room, heat and humidity are controlled by thermostatic and other apparatus, which also keeps a record. A group of workers are employed to inspect these and other temperature and humidity records and to report fluctuations outside a certain latitude. In addition, there are certain routine sequences of actions proceeding at regular intervals. The baths of sulphuric acid in the spinning room are sampled every hour. The sample is taken to the laboratory and analysed. Any fluctuation beyond certain limits is noted, and instructions delivered to the foreman in charge of the "acid house" to increase or decrease the input of sulphuric acid.

In these instances, all action is designed to produce as much rayon as cheaply as possible, within the limits of the resources of the company and the requirements of the market. These are clearly defined in a programme. The normative character of everybody's work is quite explicit in the factory. The job of the "efficiency man" in the spinning room is to approximate the process of transforming raw viscose into yarn as closely as possible to complete effectiveness, in which no machine time and no material are lost. The other control operations mentioned have the purpose of keeping the process changes and the conditions affecting those changes within a range of limits, and close to a series of constants. There is, in fact, a collection of permitted tolerances ("limits and constants") set down for all stages, which are bound together in a book. This was called the "Factory Bible" and was in the hands of every head of department. Most of the skilled work in the factory, and a good deal of the work of foremen and heads of departments, is the control of processes so that they act according to the norms laid down in the "Factory Bible." Systematic control of this order can be regarded as a series of circuits. Some are extremely short and entirely mechanical, as when a deviation from a specific temperature is corrected by a thermostat acting on the supply of hot water; some can be short and operated by a single worker, as when a clogged jet is replaced and the thread taken up and guided along its path into the spinning pot; some can be fairly complicated and involve a number of men and operations, as in the case of the routine laboratory tests.

Control procedures at the higher executive level are necessarily complex, and this is not the place to give a detailed survey of them. In this rayon factory the most elaborate of these procedures are those which relate the production process to sales requirements. At the outset of this description the receipt of orders was placed at the beginning of the whole production process as the logical precedent to it. So it is, but since the whole production process takes anything up to eight or nine days, contingencies are continually arising which make it necessary first to alter the production process, and consequently the amount or nature of the product, and second to restore production to the norm from which it departed. For example, the length of time viscose

is stored before it is spun affects its quality. Other conditions also affect quality, but are linked to the period of
storage. Tests of quality are continually made; and if the
storage period seems likely to become excessive, the usage
of viscose is speeded up by thickening the denier of yarn,
i.e., the weight per yard; this means that only the heavier
deniers ordered by the sales department are produced for a
time, and adjustments have to be made later either in the
spinning room, in the earlier parts of the process, or to sales
action itself. Most of the time of the Works Manager is
spent in reconciling actual production with maximum potential and with required production—three variables each of
which is recorded elaborately in logs, production forecasts,
weekly programmes, and reconciliation charts.

In turn, the General Manager reconciles variations in
the performance of the production departments with fluctuations in the contribution of the service and maintenance departments, chief chemist's section, personnel department,
and "reconciles" the total outcome of the works' activities
with the expectations of the head office. These expectations
are expressed as figures of programmed sales, programmed
production, and costs. (10, pp. 79–82.)

There is obviously nothing simple about this organization and the
making of the yarn. As the authors indicate, there are a great many
occasions for shifting orders and moving some things faster than others.
The "Factory Bible" is probably a very large and complicated book.
Faulty judgment or work effort on the part of anyone in the organization could put it out of whack. Yet, this is, as the authors call it, a stable
program.

The whole concern is visible as a pyramid of knowledge about the circumstances of the concern. As one descends through the hierarchy, one finds more limited information, technical and local, about these circumstances, and
also more limited control over the resources of the firm. One
also finds each person's task more and more clearly defined
by his superior, so that he is capable not only of knowing
what to do in normal circumstances without consulting anyone else, but also knows just how far he may allow a situation to depart from the normal. Beyond a certain limit he has
insufficient authority, insufficient information, and usually
insufficient technical ability to be able to make decisions. He

is informed, therefore, quite clearly when this limit occurs; beyond it, he has one course open—to report to his superior. Similarly, his part in the common purpose is defined and it is normally unnecessary for him to have to consider further how his task relates to the firm's commercial ends.

Although the specification and detachment of the individual member of the organization increases the lower down in the hierarchy he is, even the General Manager's task is carried out within the framework of a programme—indeed, of a very precisely defined programme, with uncertainties and expectations, so far as demand is concerned, ironed out for him beforehand.

The system of management within the factory was quite explicitly devised to keep production and production conditions stable. With this as the underlying principle, the system defined what information or instructions arrived at any one position in the hierarchy, what information or instructions might leave it, and their destination. Such definition was a matter of fixed, clear, and precise routine. Similarly, each working position in the hierarchy had its authority, information, and technical competence specified once for all. Moreover, since each position below the General Manager's in the hierarchy was specialized in all three features of authority, technique, and information, and nobody was empowered to act outside defined limits, all departures from stable conditions were swiftly reported upwards, and, so far as the works were concerned, the General Manager existed as the fountainhead of all information about commercial and other conditions affecting the affairs of the factory (as against technique). Such changes as did occur, therefore, were inaugurated at the top. There was, accordingly, a fairly stringent authoritarian character about the conduct of superiors to their subordinates, an authoritarianism which was accepted as reasonable, and did not in the least interfere with sociable friendliness on an equal footing on the many occasions on which members of the staff met each other outside work in the small town in which the works was located. It was perfectly possible, that is, for members of the firm to accept instruction and command as appropriate to work relationships, but to isolate these relationships from what went on outside.

What we have been considering, in this example, is the structure of management in a concern for which technical and market conditions approximated very closely to stability.

At all levels, decision-making occurred within the framework of familiar expectations and beliefs, many of which could be formulated numerically as a programme. Fluctuations in demand did occur, but these were treated as deviations from normality, and part of the task of management was to constrain the sales office in London to avoid such deviations. Production programmes, which in operational terms were planned for a week's run, were devised for monthly, three-monthly, and six-monthly periods so as to make it easier to run each weekly programme without alteration. (10, pp. 82–83)

The authors have described the very model of a highly technical, well-run, bureaucratic organization. Much classical management theory is employed in this organization. Jobs are clearly defined, as is authority. The system needs little change and little is anticipated. While suggestions for technical change may originate from below, changes involving commercial and other conditions affecting the factory are inaugurated at the top. The management and employees accept this authoritarian structure as reasonable and efficient.

In contrast let us examine a quite different company. After describing two intermediate firms, a fairly routine switch-gear operation and a less routine radio manufacturer, the authors turn to something even less routinized, an electronics plant.

Beyond this point, in the electronics industry proper, one begins to meet concerns in which organization is thought of primarily in terms of the communication system; there is often a deliberate attempt to avoid specifying individual tasks, and to forbid any dependence on the management hierarchy as a structure of defined functions and authority. The head of one concern, at the beginning of the first interview, attacked the idea of the organization chart as inapplicable in his concern and as a dangerous method of thinking about the working of industrial management. The first requirement of a management, according to him, was that it should make the fullest use of the capacities of its members; any individual's job should be as little defined as possible, so that it will "shape itself" to his special abilities and initiative.

In this concern insistence on the least possible specification for managerial positions was much more in evidence than any devices for ensuring adequate interaction within the system. This did occur, but as a consequence of a set of conditions rather than of prescription by top management. Some of these conditions were physical; a single-storeyed building housed the entire concern, two thousand strong, from laboratories to canteen. Access to anyone was, therefore, physically simple and direct; it was easier to walk across to the laboratories' door, the office door, or the factory door and look about for the person one wanted, than even to telephone. Written communication inside the factory was actively discouraged. Most important of all, however, was the need of each individual manager for interaction with others, in order to get his own tasks and functions defined, in the absence of specification from above. When the position of product engineer was created, for example, the first incumbents said they had to "find out" what they had to do, and what authority and resources they could command to do it.

In fact, this process of "finding-out" about one's job proved to be unending. Their roles were continually defined and redefined in connexion with specific tasks and as members of specific co-operative groups. This happened through a perpetual sequence of encounters with laboratory chiefs, with design engineers who had worked on the equipment the product engineers were responsible for getting made, with draughtsmen, with the works manager, with the foremen in charge of the production shops they had to use, with rate-fixers, buyers, and operatives. In every single case they, whose only commission was "to see the job through," had to determine their part and that of the others through complex, though often brief, negotiations in which the relevant information and technical knowledge possessed by them would have to be declared, and that possessed by others ascertained.

The sheer difficulty of contriving the correct social stance and the effective social manner for use in different negotiations, the embarrassment of having so to contrive, and the personal affront attached to failure to achieve one's ends by these means, induced in managers a nervous preoccupation with the hazards of social navigation in the structure and with the relative validity of their own claims to authority, information, and technical expertise.

"Normally," said a departmental manager, "management has a sort of family tree showing who is responsible for what, and what he is responsible for. It's a pity there's nothing like that here. It's rather difficult not knowing; there's a lot of trouble caused by this—you get an assistant to a manager who acts as though he were an assistant manager, a very different thing." Another man, a product engineer, said, "One of the troubles here is that nobody is very clear about his title or status or even his function." A foreman, explaining his relationship with senior managers, said of one, "It's generally gathered, from seeing T. standing about looking at the roof when something is being done to it and looking over machines, that he's in charge of plant and buildings." The same foreman, discussing his own job, said that when he had first been promoted he had been told nothing of his duties and functions. "Of course, nobody knows what his job is in here. When I was made foreman I was told to get on with the job—was just told 'You'll start in on Monday,' so I came in and started in. That was really all that was said."

The disruptive effects of this preoccupation were countered by a general awareness of the common purpose of the concern's attitudes. While this awareness was sporadic and partial for many members of the firm, it was an essential factor in, for example, the ability of the "product engineers" to perform their tasks, dependent as they were on the co-operation of persons and groups who carried on the basic interpretative processes of the concern. Indeed, discussion of the common purposes of the organization featured largely in the conversation of cabals and extra-mural groups existing among managers.

An even more important part was played by common beliefs and a sense of common purpose in the limiting case of rapidly changing conditions we encountered: a concern recently created to develop electronic equipment and components for the commercial market. While a hierarchy of management may certainly be said to have existed, positions in it were defined almost entirely in terms of technical qualifications. The conversion of this structure of technical expertise into a concern with commercial tasks required a continuous process of self education. There were two major aspects of this process. First, individual tasks in the concern were defined almost exclusively as a consequence of interaction with superiors, colleagues, and subordinates; there was no specification by the head of the concern. Secondly, this continuing definition—and redefinition—of structure depended for its success on effective communication. At the end of a discussion with senior members of staff, it was explicitly acknowledged that the organizational problems of the enterprise turned almost entirely on finding the right code of conduct which would make for effective communication—to avoid occasions, as one head of a laboratory put it, "when I'm explaining a point to a chap and he says 'Yes, yes' and I'm not at all sure whether he's caught on." (10, pp. 92–95)[2]

When the authors discussed this particular organization with a group of company presidents and government officials as an example of an "organic" rather than a "mechanistic" structure, one person observed that while it might be interesting to throw a number of people together and wait for an organization to emerge, the stringencies of economics usually prohibited one from doing so. However, the authors could point out that this firm was a part of a successful radio manufacturing company that was highly concerned with economy. The structure worked; its form of organization was as economical and specific to the tasks it had to perform as the rayon mill's form of organization. But the tasks of the two organizations were quite different.

The electronics firm violated a large number of classical principles of management. Written communications were discouraged; jobs were defined as little as possible; people found out about their jobs by defining them; interaction was face-to-face; there were numerous "hazards of social navigation"; there was considerable strain about each person's place in the organizational structure, and the personnel complained about this uncertainty. Even involvement with the goals was sporadic and partial for many members of the firm. Communication was not a matter of routing the proper information to the proper people. Rather, in this firm it was both elementary and vital to communicate by making exactly sure that the person to whom you were talking understood just what was meant.

The parallels between the two industrial firms and the two correctional institutions should be apparent. At the time it was studied, the rayon mill was dealing with a fairly stable raw material about which a good deal was known and there were fairly stable processing techniques.

---

[2] T. Burns and G. M. Stalker, *The Management of Innovation* (London: Tavistock Publications Ltd., 1961). Reprinted with permission.

Specific orders, directives, and procedures could be established. In contrast, the electronics firm, we may suspect, had very uncertain knowledge about the materials with which it dealt and the processing techniques that might be used. Therefore, a more "organic" structure was required—at least this is the name used by the authors of the study—involving a good deal of uncertainty about responsibility and tasks, but an enormous opportunity to define these responsibilities in the way that gets the job done best.

Since I have studied a similar organization in the United States, I can detail some of the uncertainties that probably prevailed. One of the constant complaints of the supervisors and engineers in the firm I studied was that when something went wrong on the production line, as it did quite frequently, they had no way of knowing just where the problem was. Sometimes sheer intuition on the part of a foreman or engineer was necessary to correct the problem. Supervisors continually asked for more information from research and development about the raw materials used in producing the electronic devices. They claimed that if they knew more about the effects of moisture or dust or temperature, or how to better analyze the materials they purchased in order to reject bad material, they could run their production more efficiently. But often they could not determine whether rejects were caused by the material, the atmosphere (such as humidity or dust), the way the worker was handling the material, or the effect of interaction among materials.

There was equal uncertainty concerning other aspects of the organization. The staff sensed that authoritarian leadership at any level was dangerous since so much initiative was required of managers. Managers and workers worked under the strain of frequent crises. If employees left in anger they were hard to replace. Yet firm technical leadership was required, not only in production, but in such areas as sales, accounting, and research and development. The "staff" functions had to be organized on an unconventional basis because of the uncertainties of production and marketing. The comptroller found himself giving evening courses to foremen so that they could use the material that the business-systems unit generated regarding costs. R and D men found themselves more or less permanently assigned to work side by side with line engineers and foremen; a line engineer might spend a good part of his time working with R and D when a new device had passed the prototype stage. Marketing men were taking technical engineering courses so that they could work with R and D and production.

These were novel experiences for the organization, and the men at the top found themselves struggling with organizational design problems. How could they keep one section of R and D free from the pressures of sales and production while they worked on somewhat "basic" research, and yet bring other sections into close contact with sales and production without diluting the autonomy of these sections? Where did sales service belong—in sales or production? Or should it be split? At the time of the study they had evolved a thoroughly decentralized operation which, in effect, created four separate small companies. Yet it appeared that even this arrangement might last only a couple of years since one product line was becoming routinized, would require less autonomy, and thus could utilize centralized staff functions.

Nevertheless, it is not possible to say that the rayon firm was well organized or that the two electronics firms were poorly organized. The electronics firms carried a high overhead in terms of costs of communication and frequent change, but it was necessary. Their technology required it. Nor would it be wise to advise the rayon firm to decentralize, increase subgroup autonomy, and change assignments and job descriptions frequently, in the interests of a more "exciting" atmosphere. The economies of a stable and efficient production system, including the investment in machinery, control techniques, job experience, communication lines, and authority structure would be endangered. Only if the technology changed radically would it be wise to alter the system.

Premature Rationalization

In this era of increasing computerization, production control measures, and time-study experts, the temptation to "rationalize" production is great. No doubt a great many firms need greater rationalization of their production methods and organizational structures. However, the preceding examples suggest that in some technological situations, the tight bureaucratic structure of the rayon mill or of the custodial institution might be quite inappropriate. Two cases of this sort are illustrative.

E. L. Trist and E. K. Bamforth (83) describe in detail an attempt to "rationalize" the operation of a coal mine in England. Engineering studies indicated that the existing system of work teams could be abandoned and much more specialization introduced into the mines. Seams could be mined by the "longwall coaling method" where economies of scale resulting from specialization could be realized. The attempt failed, however, because of the unpredictable character of coal seams and possibly because the inherent dangers in the work required an effective buddy system. The rationalization attempt broke up the existing system of interpersonal relations and mutual support and promoted expensive competition between shifts for the best seams. In general it lowered the level of cooperation and morale. Had the engineers realized the high degree of uncertainty and risk in the work—its essentially nonroutine character—they might not have been so ready to apply work-study methods.

A similar example is given by Alvin Gouldner (23) in his discussion of a gypsum mine. The plant in this case consisted of a mine which extracted gypsum and a surface plant which manufactured the raw material into wallboard. For a number of years the plant had been run on a very informal basis with leisurely lunch breaks, late arrivals and early departures, free use by employees of company materials such as dynamite and wallboard, a policy of not firing personnel, and a recruitment policy that emphasized family and friendship ties and length of residence in this semirural community.

A new manager was brought in to tighten things up and increase efficiency. While he met resistance in the surface factory, he apparently succeeded, although the author does not directly discuss this point. In the mine, however, his efforts to introduce "sound bureaucratic measures" were unsuccessful and soon abandoned. Work in the mine involved a considerable degree of personal danger and required mutual aid among the miners regardless of job assignment or status differences. There were many uncertainties concerning such matters as the placement of safety posts to hold up the roof, the best means of mining the seams, and judgments as to the most valuable seams. Because of the risk to which the men were exposed and the hard life far below the surface of the earth, the workers were accustomed to "blowing off steam" in their off-hours, and absenteeism was high. Yet the men were paid on a piece-rate basis and absenteeism did not interfere with productivity; they had apparently worked out their own arrangements to cover for their fellow workers. Thus, rules such as penalties for absenteeism were completely ineffective. Attempts to hire on a "universalistic" basis—that is, only with regard to the technical qualifications of the applicant—were also irrelevant. Miners tended to come from mining families characterized by familiarity with danger, physical strength, and respect for mutual aid. The criteria relevant to hiring surface workers were just not applicable to miners.

Conclusion

The descriptive material presented in this chapter leads to a very simple conclusion: organizations differ in their tasks, and thus in the way they are run. We contrasted two correctional institutions and two industrial firms and added a few other illustrations. "The best way" of running these organizations turned out to be quite different ways; what worked in one type would not work in another. Though simple, this lesson is so frequently ignored that it was necessary to explain it at length, with many illustrations.

But the point can be made *too* simple. Thus far it has been applied to only two types of organizations—one whose operations are quite routine and whose structure is clear and elaborate, and another with nonroutine operation and a structure which is neither clear nor elaborate. This oversimplification has resulted from reliance upon illustrations and observations rather than upon analysis, or theory. Now it is time to be much more explicit in theory and analysis. When we do, we shall see that there are more than two types of organization and that complications may arise from the fact that many organizations include both routine and nonroutine units, which must be coordinated. Thus, the next chapter will elaborate on various types of organizations and mechanisms for coordination.

But an additional task must be undertaken before this elaboration can be made. Why do routine organizations develop such elaborate structures, and why does the structure of nonroutine organizations often fail to work? What is the basis of structure in organizations? To answer this question is the next task.

Bureaucracy, Structure, and Technology

"Bureaucracy" is a dirty word, both to the average person and to many specialists on organizations. It suggests rigid rules and regulations, a hierarchy of offices, narrow specialization of personnel, an abundance of offices or units which can hamstring those who want to get things done, impersonality, resistance to change. Yet every organization of any significant size is bureaucratized to some degree or, to put it differently, exhibits more or less stable patterns of behavior based upon a structure of roles and specialized tasks. Bureaucracy, in this sense, is another word for structure.

In the last chapter we saw that structures differ greatly among organizations. Some are more bureaucratic than others. In order to understand better the variations in structure, or degrees of bureaucratization, we must understand the need for structure. The first objective of this chapter will be to show why it is not possible to have completely flexible, democratic organizations where everyone "does his own thing" in the interests of the welfare of all. Three bases for bureaucratization will be emphasized—specialization, the need to control the extra-organizational influences upon members, and the need to deal with a changing and unstable environment. Next it will be shown that bureaucratization is valuable only up to a certain point; there are some occasions when the efficiency it produces is not worth the inflexibility with which it is associated. Thus far, the analysis will in effect still be contrasting Dick and Inland, although in quite a different way from the last chapter. Once a theory about the causes of structure has been developed, other organizational possibilities will be revealed, in addition to the routine and nonroutine, bureaucratic and nonbureaucratic organizations. Various schemes, on which four types of organization are predicated, will be examined. The particular schemes and the predicted organizational consequences are less important than the general theorem: once a basis has been developed for examining varieties of organizations, it becomes possible to select the techniques which best fit any one particular organization.

The Bureaucratic Model

Why Can't There Be an Ideal Organization?

Organizations are established to produce something, such as entertainment and social interaction in the West End Ladies Monday Evening Club, foreign relations that protect our country's interests in the State Department, slim buttocks and poise in a charm school. In the process, organizations use human and nonhuman energy. This energy is utilized to transform "raw materials" into a desirable product so that people will contribute resources to the organization by paying for that product, thus making it possible for the organization to purchase more materials and labor and to continue production. There are at least two requisites in formal organization: someone at the top who determines what the product will be and allocates job assignments; and people who specialize in making some part of that product. One cannot have everyone making the evening tea or deciding what our relationship with Red China should be; a particular someone must decide that tea or relations with China are the organization's business. Specialization has a further advantage: individuals are generally incapable of performing all tasks equally well and become confused if they have to learn too many of them and do them all regularly. Their performance is better if they learn a few jobs well, especially those for which they are best suited by natural ability, training, or previous experience.

Ideally, from the point of view of efficient production, organizations should have a constant environment, and their personnel should not be influenced by extra-organizational factors. If this were the case, only the top man would have to know what the final product was. The rest would only do what they were told to do and would never question or inquire into organizational goals. Since they would do the same things over and over, they could learn every aspect of a particular job. They would purchase the supplies, keep the records, and pass on their subproduct to the next person to work on.

Personnel and the Environment

However, the ideal organization does not exist. One major reason is that the people who perform organizational tasks must be sustained by factors outside the organization. The organization is not the total world of the individual; it is not a society. People must fulfill other social roles; besides, society has shaped them in ways which affect their ability to perform organizational tasks. A man has a marital status, ethnic identification, religious affiliations, a distinctive personality, friends, to name only a few. Today it is customary to call management's attention to the fact that they are dealing with whole persons, rather than with automatons, and that therefore they should be sensitive to human relations. It is less often acknowledged, however, that a great deal of organizational effort is exerted to *control* the effects of extra-organizational influences upon personnel. Daily, people come contaminated into the organization. In this sense it is quite true that most of the problems of organizations are people problems; many of the irritating aspects of organizational structure are designed to control these sources of contamination.

Of course, organizations could not be efficient, or perhaps they could not even exist, if it were not true that people are shaped, and live, outside them. For example, society socializes individuals so that they will submit to authoritarian structures, teaches them to report to work on time, to talk, to read. This point is neither unimportant nor obvious; during many attempts to construct western-type organizations in non-western countries it has been found that non-westerners do not acquiesce in authoritarian structures, have no conception of appearing at precisely the same time every day at their work station, do not know how to converse in the logical, "straightforward" manner of western people. In our own country, part of the purpose of Head Start and other socializing programs in urban ghettoes is to prepare individuals for organizational existence. There is, apparently, no other legitimate existence in our society today.

In order to cope with the problems created by the environmental context of members, organizations have developed two methods which have nothing directly to do with the productive process itself; that is, nothing to do with the worker's tasks relating to the raw material he receives. These methods involve, first, rules and regulations and, second, staff specialists—both of which are subject to much negative comment in organizations. Of course, many rules and regulations are concerned with the productive process itself, and everyone is a specialist in an organization. But we are referring here to those rules and staff members not directly contributory to the productive process.

For example, just the simple fact that people tend to degenerate physically when they age, or may die without warning, means that some means are needed whereby successors will be available or, at least there must be criteria for hiring replacements. Ideally, each employee should perform this task for his own job—he should be in the best position to do so. But affecting the selection process are such extraneous factors as friends and relatives, bribery, spies from competing organizations, and lack of ability in judging potential successors. There may also be difficulty in finding a labor pool from which to make the selection. To solve this awkward problem organizations often hire staff specialists who decide on minimal qualifications for vacant positions and look for available people. In addition, rules may be promulgated regarding such matters as preferential treatment of relatives and conditions for advancement. The widely noted fact that top management often ignores both of these mechanisms, by hiring friends and relatives or hiring on the basis of "unscientific" screening, suggests how difficult it is to achieve controls.

In general, personnel men try to ensure, through screening devices, that the proper non-organizational characteristics are maximized in selection procedures and the improper ones minimized. Men with families are preferred because they have responsibilities and are less likely to quit when dissatisfied. Organizations in general tend toward racial, ethnic, and religious homogeneity, in part because of self-selection on the part of applicants and geographic reasons, but in part because of personnel men's attempts to limit uncertainty and increase predictability. Psychological tests are used for much the same reasons. They have been criticized, incidentally, because they may tend to ensure similar personality types because of the "self-fulfilling prophecy." That is, because these tests show that the men at the top had certain kinds of personality characteristics, it is assumed that these traits must have ensured their success. Therefore, the organization recruits or promotes only those management people who perform similarly on the tests. Since some of these subordinates inevitably reach the top when the old leaders retire, this "proves" that those with these characteristics were the most successful. Still, such tests are one way of attempting to control the problem of extra-organizational influences.

Rules and regulations, people to draft them, and others to make sure they are followed are also needed to solve the problem of personnel turnover. Joe may know his job very well and may resent any attempt to spell it out in terms of formal rules and regulations. But his successor has other characteristics which may lead him to perform it differently. The efficient organization, once it has adapted to Joe's way of doing things, either sets this down as the best and only way, to minimize adjustment problems with a new man, or, if his way does not seem the best, sets up rules to prevent the new man from repeating the error.

This example, trivial in itself, is characteristic of the proliferation of rules and staff positions in organizations: Suppose a man has a task which makes it very dangerous for him to smoke a cigarette during sequences D, E, and F, but not during sequences A, B, and C. Because of the length of time it takes a cigarette to burn or because of the possible strength of the worker's smoking habit, the organization might have to establish a rule that no smoking be done in this position because of the danger that the employee might find himself smoking during sequences D, E, and F. In this example, the organization is taking into account the extra-organizational roles and characteristics of its human members. It would also be sensible, if there were enough problems of this sort, to relieve the departmental managers of the burden of laying down such rules and to hire someone who is trained just for this sort of thing—a safety engineer, for example.

It is unnecessary to proceed in tedious detail showing how thousands of written and unwritten rules and the activities of accountants, public relations men, advertising managers, staff psychologists, physicians, and the like all serve to control the extra-organizational characteristics of employees. (Nor is this the only reason for these positions and rules.) Note, merely, that these are "nonproductive" rules and positions and one good reason why they are subject to such criticism. As more and more control must be exerted over extra-organizational influences upon behavior, more and more rules and positions proliferate to insure that control. But all this appears to be so much bureaucratic red tape, because it seems so removed from the actual tasks of the organization. "What does he know about production (or sales)?" "What has this rule to do with helping this patient?" These are familiar complaints about such aspects of bureaucracy.

Other Aspects of the Environment

All organizations, whether industrial or not, have an environment comprised, at the minimum, of suppliers; competitors; customers or clients; potential or actual unions; governmental regulatory agencies on a local, national, and sometimes international basis; new technologies; and, of course, the complex social and political milieu of the communities in which they exist. Most organizations attempt to stabilize and control these environmental influences. That is, they attempt to deal with changes in the environment by setting up rules and positions which can make it possible to deal with the environment on a routine, predictable basis. Take the simple matter of purchasing and inventory control in an industrial organization, or client-intake in a welfare organization. If the demand for goods or services were stable and could be kept stable, there would be little need for complex rules regarding the amount of inventory that must be maintained, or the provisions for purchasing, nor would there be a need for specialized positions such as purchasing agents, inventory clerks, or intake committees; once the routine was set up each person who needed a supply of materials or clients could order his own. But where demand fluctuates because the environment changes and where the output of suppliers is unpredictable, one needs complex rules for making decisions about inventory and supplies, and organizations find it worthwhile to hire specialists or to set up special committees to handle this kind of problem.

Naturally, the man who needs the supplies or clients complains about the cumbersome policies and wonders why he can't get just what he wants when he needs it. He may know that one particular kind of supply is best-suited to his particular job. Still he finds that in the distant reaches of the organization the decision is made to give him a different kind. This complicates his job and he fumes about inefficiency. However, the specialist in another part of the organization probably has decided that one supplier is more reliable than another, or that economies can result from large purchase orders, or that quality varies by suppliers and therefore, the producer may not get the precise item he wished.

One way to view staff positions is to consider them contact points with the environment—the personnel man recruits, hires, fires, and judges the labor market; the accountant deals with the intake and outflow of money; R and D units survey technical developments; marketing forecasts the demand and product changes. The people actually engaged in production and direct sales are not themselves in a position to perform these functions efficiently. Neither are they in a position to see how the labor market or the price of money is changing, nor how new technological developments will affect the firm, nor can they forecast product demands. Thus, the friction between staff positions and line positions is likely to be great.

The Need for Stabilization and Routinization

THE OPEN HOUSE

When we think of organizations we generally think of them as stable, long-lasting entities with fairly precise boundaries and with characteristics which distinguish them from all that is outside. Organizations have a location, an address. People belong to them or they do not. They go to work there for a given number of hours a day and then they leave. The organization exists on weekends and during vacation times even though most of the work force is not present. An organization appears to be separate from other things in this world.

In a sense this is a completely misleading picture of an organization. If the concept were accurate, we could safely assume that within this "house," so to speak, control is exercised over the behavior of the people who come and go within it; the walls are secure against the environment outside; the furnace is neatly equipped with a feedback system which keeps the temperature at the optimum level at all times; the lights go on and off when needed. If all this were true, organizations would be as perfect and comfortable as our homes and we could give them little thought.

However, as we have seen, people tramp in and out with mud on their shoes that they bring in from the outside world. We cannot do a perfect job of selecting the kinds of people that we do admit into the organization, and we do not retain them long enough to remake them completely. Furthermore, the windows and the doors are always open because the organization processes raw materials. It brings them in at one end, changes them, and sends them out at the other end; the process requires still other doors and windows to be opened for the reception of machinery, knowledge, and the like. Viewed in this light it is very hard to maintain control in an organization.

THE HIGH COST OF CONTROL

The devices available for maintaining control are expensive. Rules and regulations cannot possibly meet every contingency and cannot possibly avoid conflicting with one another. Every decision in an organization is a compromise because, for example, one cannot minimize employment costs and still maximize the education, training, and experience of new employees. One cannot provide adequate buffer-stocks to keep production uninterruptedly moving and at the same time keep inventory low to avoid tying up precious capital. Besides making rules and regulations, organizations hire specialists to try to keep order within this highly permeable house. Most staff specialists are in the position of trying to mediate between the conflicting demands of various parts of the organization and are thus apt to be always in hot water with one or the other, unless, of course, they have a high degree of tolerance and sophistication.

PIGEONHOLES

A third means of making the open house as secure as possible from the ravages of the environment and as stable as possible is categorization. People and things and activities are endlessly categorized, or classified, and recorded in standardized ways. He is a personnel man, not Dick Johnson. This steel is grade 9–12, not a particular piece of grade 9–12 that differs from other pieces of grade 9–12. This event calls for an authorization signed by the head of X unit in triplicate, not a particularly messy problem that McCloskey might know something about. This client falls into category 2B and thus is not entitled to such and such services without prior approval of someone at supervisory level three. Of course we violate these categorizations continually. Johnson has to be handled in a certain way; one would never take *this* kind of personnel problem to *him*. Grade 9–12 steel is very heterogeneous; it would be best to find out in which furnace it was melted before putting it on the rolling mill. Let's get hold of McCloskey and see what he says should be done, then let the authorization follow, since the head of X unit doesn't know anything about this anyway. Let's give this client these services informally; she really should not be in category 2B in this case, but we can't move her to 2A because that isn't appropriate for these other services. Categories like these take care of the vast majority of cases; if they don't, they fall into disuse. They also provide a standard by which to judge something as an exception. Besides, they are a convenient basis for disciplining someone who makes a really bad mistake. If we could not categorize, classify, and stereotype, volume production or volume services would not be possible.

Of course, all these characteristics can be stated in quite negative terms and, indeed, they usually are. Inevitably, they create problems, even though the problems they solve are more numerous and less often discussed. The rules are never fully adequate, so rules in general are deplored; the staff specialists make decisions on the basis of organizational criteria rather than subunit criteria, so the proliferation of staff and their growing power are deplored; the categories are never fully adequate, so we speak of pigeonholing and excessive paper work. All these sins can be summed up by three charges against bureaucracies: that they are inflexible, slow to act, and they resist change and innovation.

There are ready explanations for all three accusations. Most organizations are slow to act because, in order to reduce costs and reduce uncertainty, stable production runs over a long period of time have been established. To act fast and to change frequently the way things are done is to increase the cost of operating. Therefore, it may be justifiable (if conservative) to assume that the fluid and variable environment is really not so changeable after all and that many of the fluctuations may be ignored. Change is expensive. To resist change until the argument for it is overwhelming is the better part of wisdom for an organization which achieves its goals through a high volume of production.

What looks like red tape to the individual whose freedom is circumscribed appears to another individual as a perfectly appropriate protection for *his* interests and freedom of movement. As Alvin Gouldner (23, ch. 9) and Michele Crozier (13, Pt. III) have noted, rules have a double edge. They constrain the behavior of those to whom they are applied, but they also constrain the behavior of the applier. When management sets up a rule to govern the behavior of workers, management cannot ignore this rule. Thus, many rules and regulations which are tagged "red tape" may appear so only from the point of view of one of the parties involved.

People are categorized and placed into pigeonholes because it would take enormous resources to treat every case as unique and requiring thorough analysis. Like stereotypes, categories allow us to move through the world without making continuous decisions at every moment. Impersonality and formality in an organization are essential to prevent favoritism and improper discrimination, and to protect individuals from the agonies resulting from intimate knowledge and friendship when a situation demands an impersonal decision.

This is not to say that some organizations don't react too slowly, don't have improper rules or too many rules, don't categorize or pigeonhole improperly, and don't fail to see when a case really is unique. Of course rules must be changed occasionally and sometimes they are applied to the wrong situations. Of course departments and groups build empires and resist change that would be for the good of all. Of course a little bit of humanity and personal concern will grease the wheels of an organization and ease its tensions. All this is only to say that it is very difficult to maintain a good organization because of the inevitable limitations of the human and raw materials and the inevitable conflict of multiple goals. But the solution is not to do away with rules and specialists and routinization and mechanization. The answer is to continuously make these devices serve the ends you value most.

What we have described so far are the reasons for rules and regulations and staff specialists that relate to the nonproductive functions of organizations. It has been pointed out that these reasons include the need for the economies of specialization, the need to control the non-organizational or extra-organizational characteristics of staff members, and the need to adjust to changes in the organizational environment. The proliferation of staff and the elaboration of rules and formal channels are two key characteristics of what social scientists and others generally have labeled *bureaucracy*. Some use the term in its conventional sense, meaning red tape, impersonality, unwieldiness, short-sightedness. Others prefer the neutral meaning established in an enormously influential statement made by Max Weber several decades ago (89, pp. 324–340). All large-scale, complex organizations have the characteristics that Weber attributed to bureaucracy, though they vary in degree. When we turn next to the forces which make bureaucratic structures less viable, we shall be discussing "less bureaucratic" models rather than, strictly speaking, "nonbureaucratic" models. But we will conform to common usage and call them nonbureaucratic models.

For our purposes, then, the bureaucratic model refers to an organization which attempts to control extra-organizational influences (stemming from the characteristics of personnel and changes in the environment) through the creation of specialized (staff) positions and through such rules and devices as regulations and categorization. In the process of attempting to control outside influences, the bureaucratic organization seeks to stabilize and routinize its own processes in the interests of *internal* efficiency. (Overall efficiency—including the ability to adapt to external changes, such as demands for new products or services or new technologies—is a different matter.)

The Nonbureaucratic Model

The Devolution of Control

The bureaucratic organization, however, is not appropriate for all types of work. It is true that our society demands a high volume of output of standardized products—not just cars and ball-point pens, but "reformed" delinquents, penalized prisoners, utility regulation laws, doles to welfare recipients, social security checks, TV programs, and exciting football games. But it is also true that society demands continual changes in the quality, quantity, and contents of such goods. Furthermore, new goods are increasingly demanded and old ones passed over. It is not enough, any longer, simply to incarcerate and penalize offenders; there is pressure to rehabilitate or resocialize them. New technologies introduce whole new lines of products, from plastics and transistors to model-cities programs and limited-war capabilities.

Many of these changes can be readily incorporated into the bureaucratic organization—such an organization is not inflexible. The social security administration remains a bureaucracy, in our terms, even though the criteria for amounts of payment and eligibility continue to become more complex. But in some cases the rate of change is so rapid, the new techniques so unproven and so uncertain, the number of contingencies so enormous, that the bureaucratic model is only partly applicable. Equally, the bureaucratic model will not do in cases where there is no demand for or possibility of volume production as, for example, in the Supreme Court or in a company making engineering prototypes. Much routine will remain; there will always be rules and there is no demand for or possibility of volume production as, for this organization, or this part of an organization, the bureaucratic model is less applicable. Something else is needed. What is needed we will call, not surprisingly, the nonbureaucratic model.

Take the matter of safety. If new processes of transforming raw materials come so fast and change so often that very few generalizations can be made about safety factors such as smoking, protective glasses, clothing, and the use of overhead cranes, there is little reason for a sizeable staff safety function. Instead, this responsibility must be delegated to those performing the actual work. This delegation is risky; the organization loses control over standards. But in such situations those performing the actual work are in the best position to decide for themselves. The employees probably know more about the obscure and recondite dangers of the materials and the work than any safety engineer in the front office.

Or, take accounting. Perhaps because of the complex materials and supplies needed and the complex interactions between departments or between the organization and its customers or the government, no accounting rules could cover every contingency. Still, the accounting function is needed, but the large accounting office is dismantled, and its staff is dispersed to the various departments where they work closely with line officers under less rigid rules. They are likely to become intimately involved in the production process itself. Naturally, no department can be freely autonomous or independent; some generalized standard must apply to the accounting function for the organization as a whole. Still, the final product will result from a variety of systems, characterized by ingenuity, flexibility and diversity, as well as frequent change. (Under such a system, the cost of the function rises, too.)

To give some other examples: The personnel division of a company may find that the manpower requirements of the various departments are so diverse or the skills so precise that the personnel staff must continually consult with line officers. Thus, they may permit the line officers to do their own hiring, or a personnel man might be assigned to each unit, operating under the fewest possible general regulations. Again, if change is so rapid that research and development personnel must keep in constant contact with line personnel, they may find it more feasible to reassign engineers in an industrial firm, or psychologists in a clinic or hospital, or economists in a government office, to the "line" where they can work side by side with people directly engaged in the productive process.

This devolution of staff services to the line or productive function and the decreasing relevance of rules and regulations covering non-productive functions are basic characteristics of the nonbureaucratic organization. But the control problems which originally caused the creation of staff positions and rules in the bureaucratic organization do not just go away; they still have to be solved, or the cost of not solving them must be judged worth paying.

OFFSETTING INCREASED COSTS

For some organizations the problem of extra-organizational influences is minimized because of the increasing professionalization of staff members. Lengthy training and specialized skills appear to be associated with higher morale and greater commitment to organizational goals. With high morale and commitment, undesirable extra-organizational influences are minimized. An individual uses the organization as the standard by which he makes his decisions more often than he uses other criteria. Organizations which must deploy members to places where they cannot be under close surveillance (like secret agents, forest service rangers, some sales people, auto dealers) have the choice of proliferating rules and reporting procedures to keep control, or "professionalizing" such personnel so they can be trusted to act in the organization's interests. (Rules and professionalization are used together when possible since professionalization alone is risky and expensive. Not only are rangers selected and trained very carefully and through a variety of career devices tethered to the Forest Service, but they also fill out an incredible volume of reports which are scrutinized by their superiors (32). Spies are not only carefully recruited and tested, but also minutely controlled by a "handler" who can, at least in the fictional world, become something of an alter ego.) Professionalization also allows personnel to select their "type" of organization, thus minimizing the influence of incongruent extra-organizational factors. Of course, such individuals are expensive, but nonbureaucratic organizations usually charge higher prices for their goods and services than bureaucratic ones producing similar goods and services. Rates are a good deal higher in an elite psychiatric hospital than in a routine custodial institution; space capsules cost more than transport planes.

It is also possible that the costs resulting from extra-organizational factors decline proportionally as individual output increases. For example, the nonbureaucratic organization probably has far less control over the amount of time given to organizational matters. But the productivity of a high-priced scientist who puts in only five hours a day may be so great that the pay he receives for the remaining three hours when he is not working is trivial. (More likely, however, his commitment to his work, though not necessarily to the organization, is such that he puts in 10 to 12 hours a day.)

Finally, the advantages of flexibility help offset the costs associated with loss of control and loss of the advantages of specialization and high volume. If new teaching methods appear (such as programmed learning or set theory), a nonbureaucratic school can adopt them quickly and insure consumer satisfaction. It will not be necessary to dismantle a large structure which has been efficient in traditional instruction but has become cumbersome in the face of attempts to change. Its personnel will be accustomed to trying new methods and will know that the organization accepts the costs of "start-up" time and learning time when new techniques are involved. The case is even more obvious for economic organizations with low plant investment, many competing producers, and a volatile market.

Managing Change in Bureaucratic and Nonbureaucratic Organizations

Even organizations with a large volume of production can become, to a degree, debureaucratized, if the routine tasks can be transferred to machines, leaving the human members of the organization free to deal with nonroutine tasks. Thus, Peter Blau and his colleagues (5) found that a higher degree of professional training of personnel in accounting units was associated with greater use of computers. Presumably, the less-skilled people were replaced by machines. Blau also found that the span of control narrowed in the professionalized accounting units (i.e., a superior had fewer subordinates to supervise), not because the more professionalized members required closer supervision, but because they needed more interaction with their superiors. Presumably, they were dealing with more complex and nonroutine tasks which probably were not performed at all in the less professionalized accounting departments or were performed there at a low level of efficiency.

All organizations face the problem of adapting to change, but for many it may be planned and routinized, as when model changes are made in the auto industry, or else change may occur only every few years. Philip Selznick illustrates how change comes to a bureaucratic organization with his capsule account of a crisis in the Ford Motor Company:

> The organization that produced the famous "Model T" was dedicated to the goal of producing more cars per day at an ever lower cost per car. In this it was highly successful. But the organization that made this achievement possible failed to recognize or respond to changes in the market. Consumer preference was shifting to comfort, styling, and performance. By 1926, when sales were off disastrously, Ford permitted his company to engage in a national advertising campaign. He accepted this technique grudgingly, only under the pressure of a major crisis.
>
> But much more than advertising was needed to permit sales an adequate role in the organization. Design and engineering had to be influenced as well. Finally, in 1927, production of the Model T was stopped, and Ford undertook the monumental task of retooling for a completely new automobile and rebuilding factory interiors so that it could

be manufactured. It was now clear that the very techniques that brought about the great production achievement of the Model T were stumbling blocks when the need was speedy and efficient changeover. Huge, single-purpose machines had been built into production lines where more flexible machines were needed to keep up with periodic model changes. When the policy that "the customer could have any color he wanted as long as it was black" gave way to color styling, the old finishing process became completely obsolete. "Nearly every piece of the company's monolithic equipment, laid out on the assumption that the Model T would linger on forever, had to be torn down and rebuilt. The staggering changeover necessitated the replacement of some 15,000 machine tools, the total rebuilding of another 25,000, as well as the redesigning and rearrangement of $5,000,000 worth of dies and fixtures."[1] (69, pp. 109–110)[2]

A bureaucratic structure can accommodate much superficial change without altering its structure. Manufacturers of autos and appliances adjust to changing demands and occasional product improvements by routinizing change—setting up units, schedules, and programs to bring out new models on a predictable, "bureaucratic" basis. Manufacturers of household detergents periodically announce "revolutionary" or "new" products (alternating with "15¢ off") to give the impression of dynamic change, yet their adjustments in the production and marketing areas are routine. Even those two-headed relics of a Pleistocene age, the universities, committed to the preservation of knowledge and values on the one hand and to the "frontiers" of knowledge and "dynamic wellspring of change" on the other, offer new courses and programs which appear to differ little from the abandoned ones.

One gathers that most organizations, and especially the larger ones, are far more committed to the routinization of change and adjustment, with major efforts given over to "managing demand" to reduce the uncertainty of the market,[3] than they are to allowing the organization to continually change and adjust. There is very good reason for this. The nonbureaucratic organization loses economies of scale, sacrifices the

---

[1] Keith Sward, *The Legend of Henry Ford* (New York: Holt, Rinehart and Winston, Inc., 1948), p. 199.

[2] Philip Selznick, *Leadership in Administration* (Evanston, Ill.: Row, Peterson and Company, 1957), pp. 109–110. Reprinted with permission.

[3] See the acerbic remarks on this score by Galbraith (21).

advantages of specialization in personnel, programs, and equipment, incurs great costs from lack of coordination, and runs the risk of inadequate and untimely accounting information. Such an organization may even be particularly open to the exploitation of positions by managers and to empire building. Where uncertainty is high, controls weak, and performance standards uncertain, staff members have much greater leeway in exercising discretion in favor of non-organizational values and interests. From all these points of view *internal* efficiency is low as compared to the bureaucratic organization.

But internal efficiency depends on such factors as a stable market, stable technology, sufficient operational size to permit specialized centralized staff, and a sizeable labor pool of appropriate workers. Where these are absent, or where the demand for new goods and services is high, internal efficiency can be sacrificed to adaptability. Some of the tasks in a complex industrialized society have to be performed by sacrificing internal efficiency. An affluent society actually treasures some of these less efficiently produced products, whether they are needed or not. We will always have expensive couturiers producing custom clothes. Likewise, organized criminal activity will always have to be highly adaptive. Some elements in our population are willing to pay high premiums for certain goods and services that cannot be efficiently produced. Building Ferraris costs more than producing Fords.

In our public sector vested interests and political power often combine to favor short-run efficiency of routinely produced goods and services, at the expense of quality and perhaps long-range savings. It is cheaper to hand out relief checks than to organize slum dwellers to bring pressure to bear upon city hall for jobs, better housing, nondiscriminatory services, and employment opportunities. Still, relief checks appear to be costing more in the long run. Our technology for covering the land and blighting neighborhoods with concrete is routine and efficient; our technology for mass transit is primitive. We invest little in developing alternatives to mass incarceration in prisons and mental hospitals.

The Incessant Trend toward Bureaucratization

Most people who read this book would probably rather work in a nonbureaucratic organization than in a bureaucratic one. Most social scientists who write about organizations show a decided preference for the nonbureaucratic model and some hold it to be the only viable model for today's world. The nonbureaucratic organization is anti-elitist, power is less centralized, and professionals and specialists have more say. It has fewer rules, especially those governing nonproduction matters. It is more exciting, more things are happening. There is greater scope for individual responsibility at the intermediate and lower levels, and greater challenge at the top. Initiative is prized more. Yet few organizations approach this ideal; many more fit the bureaucratic model. Even those organizations which do start out as adaptive and innovative strive to rationalize and routinize. Every manager prizes freedom and initiative for himself but attempts to routinize the areas under his control. Similarly, those in control of the expanding, innovative organization appear to maximize their own freedom and rewards by making the organization itself more predictable.

Nonbureaucratic organizations which are successful grow in size and stability; introduce economies of scale and complex control devices; reduce the skill level or introduce ever more laborsaving, efficient machinery; attempt to manage demand through advertising, monopoly, and collusion to stabilize their environment; and eventually they become profitable and bureaucratic. One of the most frequently posed questions in successful, growing concerns is, "How can we keep the *esprit de corps,* the flexibility, the excitement, the identification with the organization as we grow larger"? The question is asked as frequently in the firm with 100 employees that must add 20 as it is in the firm with 1000 that must add 200. "I no longer know the people here," the president, and then the vice-president of operations, and then the department head complain. But not only increased size (though this is important) but also rules and specialties are needed as control is sought to increase predictability and, presumably, profits. These are the factors which limit face-to-face interaction, a sense of mission, and flexibility.

For example, the innovating psychiatric clinic gains a reputation and attracts both patients and personnel. Its novel techniques, created by one or a few people, are viewed as the reason for its success. Thus, the same techniques are prescribed for new personnel to follow. As a result, these techniques must be explicated and broken down into steps, and checkpoints must be provided along the way. Soon the new approaches are frozen into convenient dogma, and the clinic has become a factory. Perhaps it no longer produces the results that it once did, when the personal qualities of the few innovators infused the techniques. But since few consumers (clients) or referral sources can really judge the quality of service anyway, the institution's reputation survives for some time, perhaps until a couple of new people, discouraged by the dogma and bureaucracy, start their own clinic and the cycle is repeated.

The successful small law firm, blessed with one or two imaginative people and probably some very good connections and publicity, adds staff and clients, and becomes a routinized giant in its field. The greatest threat to successful, small advertising agencies is the need to balance growth with flexibility. Growth can be phenomenal since clients bring in huge advertising programs that will run for a few years. "We grew too fast," is the common complaint. "But we had to; our old accounts would not stay with us unless they were reassured by our getting huge new accounts," is the next line. The inventor of a sophisticated electronic device has but two choices—to sell the invention to a large firm, or to build his own large firm, with volume production. The company must be large because you cannot market one model of a transistor, or integrated circuit, or camera, or copying machine. At the very least, you need various models and related lines in order to justify the sales and marketing expenses. But it is hard for the inventor to step aside and leave his company to others while he invents yet another device. So he sells this invention or builds or joins a large bureaucracy.

Of course there are ways of minimizing these trends while still retaining the profits and prestige of high-volume production and standardized quality. Innovative units can be somewhat protected from routine ones. Product groups can be formed which operate to some degree like small independent companies. The boss, like Edwin Land of Polaroid, can have his own lab adjoining his office. The production of goods or services can be dispersed geographically (a branch of the clinic or a separate office of the law firm can be set up). But these and other devices carry price tags that are calculable (as well as many that are incalculable), whereas the advantages of the efforts are almost always incalculable. It is hard to calculate morale and flexibility. And in organizations, the calculable carries more weight than the estimate.

Thus, the thrust is to routinize, limit uncertainty, increase predictability, and centralize functions and controls. Whether the lure is security, power, growth, or profits, and whether the field is government, industry, culture, or welfare, bureaucratization proceeds apace. Old giants may stumble or crumble and give way to nonbureaucratic Davids, as happened when the trucks challenged the railroads or as might happen some day as poverty programs challenge the established "welfare industry." Still, the trucking industry is now increasingly rationalized and centralized, and poverty programs may be replaced by an efficient, bureaucratic minimum-income program for all family units. The non-bureaucratic organization is aptly called by some a "problem-solving" organization, as contrasted to a production organization. But when the problems are solved, mass production begins. The resulting organization may not be the same one whose job is production, but it is bound to be a much larger entity than the R and D or engineering prototype organization which can afford the nonbureaucratic structure.

More Complex Models

By now, the reader may have become irritated because we have been speaking of two types as if there were only two types, and "the" organization as if it were a pure example of one or the other of the types. Actually, of course, the terms "bureaucratic" and "nonbureau-cratic" are only crude extremes. Not only might there be many shades of grey between the two, but, as we shall see, there may be alternative forms which are not even on that continuum or line running from bureaucracy to nonbureaucracy. More important for present purposes, however, is the possibility of using both types of structure in the same organization.

The Mixed Model

Let us assume, for a moment, that we are talking about organizations where all three of the following functions are important: research, production, and marketing. Though industrial terminology is being used here, it should be recognized that all organizations have, to at least some limited extent, all these functions. A correctional institution, an employment agency, the social security administration, or various military units all not only produce products but must also market them in some form or other. The manner in which they produce and market these products is based upon an appropriate technology. To find, change, develop, and improve the technology constitutes a research function, as does the determination of what the new products will be. Of course, for some organizations, marketing is a minor problem, while for others it is a major one, and the same is true of research and even of production. Assuming all three are important, however, how should they be organized?

The organizational form will depend upon the state of the art in each function and the changes required by the environment. Preferably production and marketing would be routinized; even fairly routine research functions would be preferred. In his theory of industrial capitalism, the economic historian Joseph Schumpeter (66, p. 132) built his central argument around the concept of "the routinization of innovation." He argued that large firms with extensive resources could produce new products and devise new methods of making them almost on a routine basis. But it is hard to conceive of an assembly-line R and D unit, though some operate far more routinely than others. Sales and production, on the other hand, can be either highly routine or nonroutine. If all three are routine (or nonroutine), the organization has little difficulty in determining the best method of organizing the whole. All can be structured alike and integration problems are minimized.

However, it is far more common to find varying degrees of routinization among the three functions. Typically, production is fairly routine and exists in a stable environment; research is nonroutine; and marketing is in-between. This situation presents problems of coordination beyond those normally encountered when there are different units, since the three units will think differently and will be accustomed to different ways of getting things done. Production, for example, may think only in terms of the very short run. This is the basis upon which this function is judged; the unit is not responsible for, nor in a position to anticipate, new products or techniques. Marketing, however, must take a somewhat longer perspective. (If the marketing function is not developed, and only a sales division exists, its perspective may be as short-range as production.) Development, and especially research, however, should have a relatively long perspective compared to production and marketing. Time perspectives establish priorities, and thus the units may clash. They will disagree about such matters as the allocation of resources or the urgency of solving a particular problem. Not only perspectives are involved, but also actual structures. With its short-range perspective and precise goals which can be measured, production is likely to have highly specialized subunits, clear lines of authority, precise rules and procedures. Research, at the other extreme, may depend more upon lateral and diagonal communication among its members, resulting in a good deal of informal contact; there may be few intermediate measures of productivity and few binding rules or procedures. It may be difficult for members of these two departments to work together, or even to communicate information easily, because of their different "styles."

Lawrence and Lorsch (36), in an important book, have studied this problem in detail in six plastic firms, where the market and technology changed rapidly. Here they found quite different time conceptions and goal orientations among production, marketing, and R and D. These differences inhibited coordination and cooperation between the units. R and D would complain, for example, that neither marketing nor production had a sufficiently long-run view. From marketing they needed to know what were the future demands of customers rather than present ones; from production, they needed to know the extent of flexibility available for future production changes rather than the difficulties encountered with the new item just introduced. Production, of course, was much more concerned with the here and now, since sales was breathing down their necks. The three units were also different in their structures. Since production was the most bureaucratically organized and research the least, problems ensued. For example, the production manager complained that those responsible for coordinating production and R and D constantly came to him about matters that should have been handled by people several layers above him in the production hierarchy. But the coordinators, in this case identified with the research department, were accustomed to direct contact and on-the-spot problem solving in their department, regardless of formal rank. They could not understand why the production manager insisted upon going through channels. He, on the other hand, could not understand how he could be expected to violate rules and procedures so casually. The problem was not a matter of personality or daring, but one of coordinating two quite different structures. In the production manager's view, most of his work had to be handled through channels and by following the rules and procedures; only in this way could the unit run smoothly on a high-volume, low-cost basis.

Significantly, the most successful of the firms were those in which the three functions were most distinctive, as well as the most integrated. As conceptualized by Lawrence and Lorsch, integration did not mean a fusing together of the various units, thus minimizing differences and producing a common, bland outlook, even though such a result would appear to be the common sense goal. Rather, their view of integration was to allow each department to be as different in its outlook and structure as its tasks demanded—that is, to be highly distinctive—but to utilize mediating devices that stood midway between the outlook of any two departments. The more successful firms used mediating units (such as committees, *ad hoc* groups, assigned "integrators") which were not dominated by the perspective of either of the two groups. If production's perspective was short-term while research took the long view, the mediating individual or unit required a middle-range perspective.

The wisdom of such an arrangement is in recognizing that both perspectives are legitimate, that different structures can exist within the same firm, or that a bureaucratic structure is as appropriate for some tasks as a nonbureaucratic structure is for other tasks. To accept such differentiation within an organization appears to be a problem for many top executives. On the face of it, coordination would be more easily achieved if all units were structured alike and all were imbued with the same perspectives regarding goals, time, authority. The research of Lawrence and Lorsch, in which they refer to the "contingency model" of organizations (where structures are contingent upon, or depend upon, the nature of the tasks with which they are meant to deal) challenges this obvious approach.

One suspects that many top executives intuitively recognize the importance of allowing differentiation to flourish to some extent and see the need for units to be structured differently. If things are going smoothly, they will leave well enough alone and attribute the success of the units to "good leadership." However, when top executives must make important decisions, as when new appointments must be made, or the firm is in trouble, or new units have to be set up (for example, separating research from development), few are willing to risk differentiation at the expense of presumed integration. If new products lag, the response may be to tighten up the structure of research, since that arrangement works so well in production. If a marketing unit is to be added to, or separated from, the sales department and given new resources, who else should head it but the successful head of the sales unit? If the new computer has worked wonders with production costs through an elaborate inventory and costing program, why not expand the program to the development unit?

In all these cases the assumptions of "one best way" or "leadership qualities" or "obvious administrative principles" are involved. The assumption is that what worked in one place will work in another and will bring about homogeneity or integration or reduce conflict. Yet tightening up the hierarchy in research will probably impede the flow of ideas and willingness to experiment. Research is always risky and uncertain. Nor is the successful head of sales necessarily fitted to understand the different time span, goals, performance criteria, or work cycle of marketing. He may be able to do so, but his success in sales is no guarantee. A "real-time," "on-line" inventory and accounting system that works for production is likely to jam up the works in the development unit where allocations are hard to make, mistakes must be covered up, or supplies must be quietly "banked" in anticipation of furious activity when a breakthrough seems imminent. Only those at the lower levels of management in the development unit are likely to know what to horde or what brands should be avoided despite quantity discounts.

The advantage of making such a view explicit should be mentioned. Too often the executive intuits such truths and may even be disposed to apply them in crisis situations. Since he lacks a rationale and a vocabulary, however, he is forced to give essentially irrelevant justifications. It is probably true, but irrelevant, that managers in the development unit would sabotage the new accounting system without giving it a chance, and thus it should not be extended there. This reasoning does a disservice to that unit and paints a picture of irresponsible individualists who do not have the interests of the firm at heart. How much better to say that the nature of the unit's work would make such a system a hindrance rather than a help. Why not explain that, while the system could be installed and operated, it would centralize decisions that have to be made at a lower level and would thus reduce flexibility? Rather than saying that the research manager has done a good job in research, but would not do well if moved to production because he has never been a foreman on a production line or because his personality isn't suited to the job, why not say that we need someone with experience in making a chain of command do the job it is meant to do, rather than someone skilled at "scrambling"? All types of leaders can be given their due, while the personality or the uncalloused hands of the research man are not maligned. It is good to do the right thing even if the wrong reasons are given; but to do the right thing and also make explicit the correct reasons reinforces the act and makes similar actions more feasible in the future. Sometimes the reasons for an action have more consequences than the action, for they indicate the criteria which will be used in the future, permitting others to make the appropriate adjustments.

Information relating to the departmentalization and integration of nonprofit organizations is not as detailed as research on profit-making firms, yet one would suspect that the same principles hold true. Classroom teaching may be routine in a school, whereas counseling and guidance and work with groups in the environment may not. The R and D units in the military establishment may be quite nonroutine, yet they may have to articulate closely with operational units. More and more, the military have assumed political functions which presumably should be organized on a different basis from the work of tactical units; yet both kinds of units must work closely together. The clinical staff in a correctional institution and the custodial staff have similar problems of integration. In matters of university policy the operating structure and outlook of engineering schools and humanities divisions would differ; therefore, only the most general form of organization should be imposed on both. Yet despite these differences, some articulation and cooperation are needed.

These distinctions within organizations are not unchanging. Suppose that a traditional, bureaucratic public school runs into trouble because of the changing character of the district it serves and finds that it must modify its instructional program. It may decide to take out of the bureaucratic structure (which heretofore characterized the whole organization) one unit which will experiment with different programs, at the same time gradually introducing new personnel for the new venture, since existing personnel are less open to a new viewpoint. In such a situation, a period of disorganization and dissatisfaction in the new unit can be expected until the transferred personnel become adjusted to the different task and structure in the new unit. Then links will have to be built between the new unit and the rest of the school to bring about gradually the desired instructional changes. Note that the school as a whole need not change its structure—the new programs can be efficiently run on a bureaucratic basis, but when they are new they must be handled as such. Once the unit has introduced and gained acceptance for the programs, the organization is stable again and the unit may be absorbed into existing units.

However, more than the instructional program is likely to change. New "marketing" and "purchasing" programs must also be introduced. What was once a stable relationship with, say, a middle-class neighborhood now becomes an uncertain relationship with a neighborhood that is becoming working class and may have changed its racial and ethnic characteristics. In the past, the middle-class principal and teachers were easily able to handle the relationships with middle-class parents and the other agencies which dealt with the school. But with the change in the "raw material" to be processed, uncertainty is introduced, and there may be a change in demands of the "consumers"—not only the parents, but also the police, local government, and social work agencies. While the school may remain bureaucratic and routine (it is difficult otherwise to process a large number of youthful humans who, regardless of their class or race, will be recalcitrant, self-activating, unwilling "members" of the organization), a new unit set up to handle relationships with the environment will be quite nonroutine in its operations and (if the principal has any organizational wisdom) nonbureaucratic in structure. What may seem like rule-violation privileges for members of the unit (among teachers, even the right to arrive late or leave early, because of off-grounds assignments, can cause resentment) is merely a different form of organizational behavior—and often a much more demanding one.

It might appear that nonbureaucratized units appear only at the fringes of an organization—research units, special service units, and the like. They often do serve to deal with the unstable and uncontrollable environment, as contrasted to the more controllable production function. But even production functions can vary within organizations. In hospitals, for example, obstetrics and gynecology is a relatively routine department, which even has something resembling an assembly (or deassembly?) line wherein the mother moves from room to room and nurse to nurse during the predictable course of her labor. It is also one of the hospital units most often accused of impersonality and depersonalization. For the mother, the birth is unique, but not for the doctor and the rest of the staff who go through this many times a day. At the other extreme, perhaps, is cardiac surgery, especially where open-heart surgery or organ transplants are done. The remaining nursing or medical units can be fairly easily deployed upon a scale of routineness or nonroutineness. Yet, in the vast majority of hospitals, nursing organization, rules, regulations, and staffing patterns for markedly different units are the same for all. Whereas only a few registered nurses are required in the routine units—practical nurses or nurses aides can be used instead—while many registered nurses are necessary in nonroutine units, such patterns are rarely found. The proportion of registered nurses to other nursing personnel is either kept equal for all departments or decided upon political grounds—e.g., the power of certain doctors.

No more wisdom is shown by many industrial corporations in managing their engineering units. A prestigious corporation will seek to recruit from the top 10 or 15 percent of top engineering schools, but much of their engineering work is likely to be routine and to require little imagination. The ability of the top students who get these assignments will be wasted, and they are likely to sour and leave. They are also paid top prices for work which could be performed by an average student at an average price. Some engineering units attempt to systematically discriminate between routine and nonroutine units and to make assignments accordingly, but most do not appear to do so.

Technology Models

So far we have been content with a simple polar contrast between bureaucratized organizations or units and nonbureaucratized units. The key to the distinction has been the kind of work performed in the organization or unit of the organization: its degree of routine or lack of routine. But if we analyze the term "routine" more closely, it appears that we mean that two conditions are present—there are well-established techniques which are sure to work, and these are applied to essentially similar raw materials. That is, there is little uncertainty about methods and little variety or change in the tasks that must be performed.

Similarly, nonroutineness means that there are few well-established techniques; there is little certainty about methods, or whether or not they will work. But it also means that there may be a variety of different tasks to perform, in the sense that raw materials are not standardized, or orders from customers ask for many different or custom-made products.

The operations of some firms may have little variety, yet quite a bit of uncertainty; others may have little uncertainty, but a great deal of variety. These two types are neither highly routine nor highly nonroutine. They are in the middle somehow, but they are not in the same middle; they themselves differ from one another. So it is possible to be nonroutine in one sense and not another, or routine in one sense but not in another. This possibility will be explored in this section. Let us begin at the beginning, however, with technology and raw materials and pursue the above distinction in more detail.

VARIABILITY AND SEARCH

As noted earlier, organizations are designed to get some kind of work done. To do this work they need techniques or technologies. These techniques are applied to some kind of "raw material" which the organization transforms into a marketable product. It doesn't matter what the product is; it may be reformed delinquents, TV programs, advertising symbols, governmental decisions, or steel. But some technology is required, not only in the actual production process, but also for procuring the input of materials, capital, and labor and disposing of the output to some other organization or consumer, and for coordinating the three "functions" or "phases" of input-transformation-output.

How does one think about, or conceptualize technology so that it may be analyzed in this way, as a means of transforming raw materials (human, symbolic, or material) into desirable goods and services? In this

view of technology, machines and equipment are merely tools; they are not the technology itself. Indeed, the personnel man uses a technology that has little to do with tools. Nor can we use the actual techniques such as are found in production manuals, for these are too specific to the particular organization. Instead, let us consider the individual who is assigned to do a specific task.

He receives stimuli (orders, signals) to which he must respond. Even the decision to ignore the stimulus or not even to "see it" is a response. He "searches" his mind to decide what kind of a response to make. So far we have two concepts with which to work: the stimulus and the response. The response is conceived of as "search behavior": If the stimulus is familiar and the individual has learned in the past what to do in the face of it, little search behavior is required. He may respond automatically or after a moment's thought. The response may be to turn to a pile of instructions, manuals, a computer, or a clerk, but the problem with which the stimulus presents him is "analyzable"; there are known ways of solving it, and little reflection or judgment is required after one has some experience with it. No two stimuli are ever exactly the same, of course, and as living beings we do not respond to them as automatons. But, in the technical jargon, we make "incremental adaptations from existing programs or portions of existing programs" to standardize the new situation.

If the stimulus is unfamiliar, however, and the individual decides not to ignore it or to panic, considerable search behavior must be instituted, and the search is of a different kind. The problem presented by the stimulus is not immediately analyzable; search must take place without manuals, computers, or clerks who have the requisite information and programs. The individual must rely upon a residue of something we do not understand at all well—experience, judgment, knack, wisdom, intuition. Nonroutine tasks are of this sort—the problems call for "unanalyzable search procedures."

If we substitute a more general term for stimuli—raw material—we can see that the nature of the search procedure depends a good deal upon what is known about the material that one is to transform through techniques. If a good deal is known that is relevant to the transformation process, search can be quite routine and analyzable. If you perceive a delinquent as simply lacking in respect for adults because he has never been made to obey adults, your way is clear. The raw material is simple and known, and the techniques are readily available from military or prison history, if nothing else. If you perceive delinquents as complicated, self-activating, unique individuals about whom not a great deal is known, search is unanalyzable and must rely upon vague processes, such as empathy, understanding, or interpreting early childhood experiences.

The other dimension of technology which will be used here is the variability of the stimuli presented to an individual—the variety of problems which may lead to search behavior. Sometimes the variety is great and every task seems to be a new one demanding the institution of search behavior of some magnitude (whether analyzable or unanalyzable). Sometimes stimuli are not very varied and the individual is confronted chiefly with familiar situations and few novel ones. Note that, in industrial firms, this is not necessarily a distinction between a great or small variety of products. Automobile firms produce an amazing variety of models and a staggering variety of parts, but these are not novel situations requiring search behavior (except in the design and engineering of model changes).

Note also that the difference between analyzable or routine search and unanalyzable search procedures is not necessarily the same as the distinction between technologically advanced and technologically backward industries. Some semiconductors, such as auto diodes, are a product of advanced technology but they can be made in a quite routine fashion. Certain kinds of ferro castings for the auto industry—a technologically "backward" process—cannot be made on a routine basis. To routinize production would require the solution of problems that have yet to be analyzed.

We now have two dimensions, the degree of variability of stimuli and the degree to which search procedures are analyzable. Let us refer to the first as simply the number of *exceptions* encountered by the individual. If we dichotomize and then cross-classify these there are four possibilities which, in Figure 1, we have labeled craft, nonroutine, routine, and engineering.

A factory manufacturing a standard product like heating elements for electric stoves (cell 4), and an engineering firm building made-to-order machines such as drill presses or electric motors (cell 3), may both be routine to the extent to which search behavior is analyzable. Still, they differ in the variety of occasions when search must be instituted—rarely in the factory, and quite frequently in the engineering firm. The engineering firm must continually modify designs and introduce modifications to meet the customers' needs. In a firm making fine glassware (cell 1), search may be as unanalyzable as in the factory which makes nuclear-propulsion systems (cell 2). Yet the variety of the stimuli in the

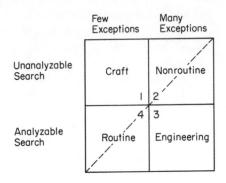

FIGURE I.   *Technology variables.*

glassware factory is small, while the varying requirements of the customers of the other firm present a great variety of problems or stimuli.
The work of the nuclear fuel system firm would be highly nonroutine,
combing unanalyzable problems with great variability of problems; the
operations of a heating-element factory or a mill making reinforcing
bars for concrete structures would be highly routine—a small variety of
problems, while those which do occur would be subject to analyzable
search procedures. The glass firm is low on variability but high on
unanalyzable search procedures (therefore, referred to as a craftsman
model). The engineering firm is high on variability but has analyzable
search procedures—an engineering model.

Note that if one were discussing only routine and nonroutine
companies or bureaucratic and nonbureaucratic structures, only cells 4
and 2 would be relevant. These are represented by a two-dimensional
continuum characterized by a broken line; this is the sort of operation to
which we have previously limited our discussion. However, organizations can fall into the categories represented by cells 1 and 3 though
they probably would cluster rather close to the center of the figure.

The same kind of analysis can be used for people-changing organizations. Now let us use as criteria the nature of the raw material instead
of search procedures (Figure 2). In the case of cells 1 and 2, the
perceived nature of the raw material is not well understood, while it is
well understood in cells 3 and 4. In the case of cells 1 and 4, the
material is perceived as uniform and stable, that is, there is variability,
whereas in cells 2 and 3 the material is nonuniform and unstable, with

	Uniform and Stable	Nonuniform and Unstable
Not well Understood	Socializing institutions (e.g., some schools) 1	Elite psychiatric agency 2
Well Understood	Custodial institutions, vocational training 4	Programmed learning school 3

FIGURE 2. *Raw material variables (people-changing examples).*

high variability. Cell 1 relates to socializing institutions; for example, some types of public schools. Here little is known about the methods of socializing children; all are treated as similar. In contrast, in cell 3, if the revolution in programmed learning ever really succeeds, schools are possible which utilize programmed-learning techniques almost exclusively. Here it is assumed that a great deal is known about the nature of the raw material, that is, we know just how to get people to learn because we know about cognitive processes and can design teaching machines to tap these processes. But our increasing knowledge about people indicates that they really differ considerably. Some learn fast and some learn slowly. Some are good at math and others at reading. Therefore, the children are perceived as not uniform. Different programs must be designed for different types of pupils. It is also possible that they will be perceived as rather unstable. Therefore the machines must correct for this characteristic (or they must signal a human instructor who will enter on occasion to deal with the occasional reactions of people who sit in front of teaching machines for a long time).

Cell 2—the elite psychiatric agency—might well be the institution called Inland in the last chapter; cell 4 might be the institution called Dick. The Inland staff believed that they did not understand children too well. That is, a great deal of search behavior was necessary in dealing with the problems which arose in the school. The staff had to be quite adaptive. They also believed that children varied widely and were potentially unstable. It was impossible to predict how they were going to behave. At Dick, however, delinquents were perceived as uniform and stable (with the appropriate degree of repression the children could be kept under control and that was all that was necessary). There the techniques of change were fairly well understood. The children needed discipline and to learn to respect adults.

TECHNOLOGY AND STRUCTURE

What, then, does technology have to do with the *structure* of the organization? The answer has already been strongly hinted at in the discussion of nonbureaucratic and bureaucratic structures. But now it is possible to be a little more specific. We must assume here that, in the interest of efficiency, organizations wittingly or unwittingly attempt to maximize the congruence between their technology and their structure. Many which fail to make such a match should be more or less bureaucratically organized than they are. But let us assume that they have all studied the sociology of complex organizations and have adapted their structures to fit their technology. What would the four types of firms look like?

There are many, many ways to conceptualize structure. For our purposes here let me choose the following variables: the discretion of subgroups; their power; the basis of coordination within a group; and the interdependence of groups. For the moment, let us also deal only with production, although these concepts are equally applicable to marketing and perhaps even to the research aspects of organizations. If we single out middle and lower management we can make some predictions about the organization of each group and the relationship between them. Middle management here will, in general, mean the people who are concerned with the administration of production; we will call this the technical level. Lower management is concerned with the supervision of production.

Figure 3 suggests some of the structural characteristics of the four types of firms. In the nonroutine type of firm—characterized by unanalyzable search procedures and the need to deal with many exceptions—both discretion and power are high in both groups; in both, coordination is through feedback (mutual adjustment) rather than through advance planning (programmed), and finally, the interdepen-

	Discretion	Power	Coordination within Groups	Interdependence of Groups	Discretion	Power	Coordination within Groups	Interdependence of Groups
Technical	Low	Low	Plan		High	High	Feed	
				Low				High
Supervision	High	High	Feed		High	High	Feed	
			Decentralized				Flexible, polycentralized	
				1	2			
				4	3			
Technical	Low	High	Plan		High	High	Feed	
				Low				Low
Supervision	Low	Low	Plan		Low	Low	Plan	
			Formal, centralized				Flexible, centralized	

FIGURE 3. *Task structure. Task-related interaction.*

dence of the groups is high. What this means is that the supervisors of production work closely with the technical people in the administration of production since the latter cannot call the shots for the former on the basis of routine information sent upstairs. Indeed, job descriptions may be such that it is difficult to distinguish the supervisory level from the technical level. Both groups are free to define situations as best they can. Therefore, both have considerable power with respect to such matters as resources and organizational strategies.

This model resembles what others have called the organic as opposed to the mechanistic structure, or the professional or collegial as opposed to the bureaucratic structure. This type of structure is probably efficient only for highly nonroutine organizations. There are few of these, even though they are quite visible and attractive to social scientists who see in them reflections of their academic institutions and values.

Most firms fit into the quite routine cell. It is in their interest to fall in this category because it means greater control over processes and much more certainty of outlook (we are ignoring market situations). In routine firms, the discretion allowed to both supervisors of production and administrators of production is minimal—there is little ambiguity in these situations. The power of the technical middle-management level, however, is high, for it controls the supervisory level on the basis of routine reports. In both cases coordination within the levels comes through planning (giving further power to the technical level) because events can be foreseen. Interdependence between the two groups is likely to be low. This arrangement approaches the bureaucratic model. Where it is appropriate, it is undoubtedly the most efficient.

In the engineering model—characterized by analyzable problems with many exceptions—the technical-level functions more like the nonroutine firm. There is great discretion in choosing among programs, and considerable power, and coordination is achieved through the feedback of information for problem solving. But on the shop floor, discretion and power are—should be—minimal. Planning is the basis of coordination here, and there is little interdependence between the two levels—designs are sent down and executed. In the craftsman model—characterized by unanalyzable problems and few exceptions—it is the supervisory level which has discretion and high power and coordinates through feedback. The technical level is weak, responds to the supervisors of production, and needs little discretion and little power. Coordination is on the basis of planning in the technical level. Interdependence of the two levels can be low.

To become even bolder in our speculation, Figure 3 may be revised to include two more unusual types of industrial organizations—the research and development firm or unit, which would be very nonroutine, and the continuous processing industry, such as oil or chemicals, or, to some extent, beer and other beverages, which would be very routine. Other examples of craft and engineering firms can also be added. (See Figure 4.)

The elliptical character of the model suggests that it is somewhat unusual to find organizations at the extreme of the axis represented by the dotted line. Still, examples do exist on that continuum. The distinction is not simply between routine and nonroutine or between bureaucratic and nonbureaucratic, as represented by the broken line.

This analysis is, admittedly, entirely speculative.[4] However, research is proceeding along these lines, and there may be some support

---

[4] For technical articles discussing these ideas see Perrow (56, 57, 58).

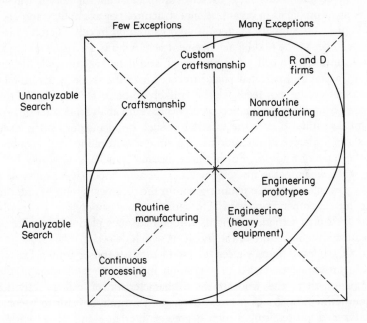

FIGURE 4.

for the specific models and predictions. We have gone into this particular theory in such detail in order to suggest at least one way of conceptualizing differences among organizations and to show that these differences indicate different kinds of strategies, none of which are either good or bad in themselves. As noted, most social scientists consider the nonbureaucratic, or nonroutine organization to be good and the bureaucratic or routine organization to be bad (it impedes progress, is old-fashioned, is hard on its employees, etc.).[5] But this judgment is debatable. One of the purposes of the R and D firm, or the nonroutine organization, is to generate ways of routinizing production and building better bureaucratic controls into organizations. Furthermore, for routine work, the bureaucratic structure may be both the most efficient and the most humane. Not all people prefer the hectic, open-ended, and uncertain character of nonroutine tasks, not even top management.

[5] For example, see Bennis (3), McGregor (44), Likert (38), Gouldner (23), Crozier (13), and V. Thompson (82).

In addition, this little exercise in speculation suggests a way of looking at problems in organizational structure. For example, going back to Figure 1, to simplify matters, if an organization in cell 1 (craft) hires an engineer at the middle-management level who is used to working in an organization in cell 3 (engineering), and if he tries through the use of discretion and personal power to coordinate the work in his unit by means of on-the-spot feedback, he is likely to be in for trouble. In this type of firm, many production problems have no analyzable solution. An engineer cannot dictate the solution of such problems nor can he exercise a high degree of discretion in helping or controlling staff members at the supervisory level. Furthermore, because problems vary very little and exceptional occasions seldom occur, he will find that he must do a great deal more advance planning within the technical group in order to support the supervisory level. He cannot expect supervisors to coordinate their own activities primarily through advance planning because of the unanalyzable nature of the problems which do occur.

Or, suppose that a successful production supervisor from a firm in cell 4 (routine) is moved to a position in a different division of the company where the work is more characteristic of cell 2 activities (nonroutine). Such a supervisor might find it quite difficult to become accustomed to exercising a high degree of discretion and power within this supervisory level. He might also be unable to adjust to coordination achieved through on-the-spot discussion when he has been used to coordination by means of fairly routine advance planning.

However, these examples relate to the problems of individuals. A more striking instance might be a case involving the recommendations of a management consultant firm which is accustomed to dealing with organizations within cell 4 (routine). Should the consultants try to apply their customary solutions to an organization in one of the other cells, they well might fail. (The Hoover Commission, charged with reorganizing much of the federal government, consistently made this error.) Similarly, a management-training program designed to increase the independence and autonomy of managers and the interdependence of groups could be quite successful in cell 2 (nonroutine), but be a waste of time in cell 4. To cite a final example: We have noted that organizations may attempt to move into cell 4 by reducing the number of exceptions that may occur, by decreasing the variability of raw materials, and by finding analyzable ways of solving their problems. However, this victory may be short-lived. If the market suddenly changes, or the technology changes, such an organization may find itself back in cells 3, 2, or 1. It would be well to be prepared to change the organizational structure when such events occur.

More important than the specific examples or recommendations, however, is the perspective illustrated here. This view holds that organizations are not all alike and that the way in which they may vary is in terms of their technology. Two aspects of technology—exceptions and search—are abstracted and analyzed independently and concurrently. Whether or not the scheme just presented is verified by empirical research, and whether or not it proves to have predictive value, matters less than this: before an organization's problems can be solved, it is essential to determine the nature of the organization. Once the determination is made, some administrative and management proverbs may apply very well but others may be irrelevant or even invalid.

The social-structural view of organizations is only beginning to generate such perspectives. To add to the few now current, many more will probably develop in time. Any two may have a compelling logic in themselves but may not be compatible with each other. This should not cause great alarm, since an organization can generally be viewed from several quite different viewpoints or positions and each can yield some useful truths.

THE WOODWARD MODEL

For example, the first major attempt to apply a technological perspective to organizations differs in several respects from the one just outlined but is quite viable in its own right. In addition, it touches upon some important practical matters not covered by the previous scheme. Joan Woodward (94), working at the time out of a technical college in South Essex, England, conducted a study of 100 firms in an industrial area in attempting to test the utility of "classical management theory." She was interested in such matters as ideas concerning types of organizational structure (functional, line, or line-staff); degree of specialization of functions; the optimum span of control and number of hierarchical levels; and staff-worker ratios. None of these factors had any particular significance in relation to organizational success. As she says, this was a disconcerting finding for a group attempting to teach management principles in a technical college. Only after the firms were grouped according to their typical mode of production did the data fall into place. In its most simplified form she uses three types of production systems: unit and small-batch (e.g. made-to-order items, such as custom suits, prototype electronic equipment, custom furniture, and machine tools), large-batch, assembly, and mass production (e.g. large bakeries, mass-produced clothing, industrial equipment, autos), and process production (e.g. oil, chemicals, and pharmaceuticals). Simply stated, the three systems may be called unit, mass, and process. She describes the whole scale as roughly equivalent to increasing technical complexity, or technical advance in historical terms.

Considered in this way it appeared that firms with similar production systems had similar organizational structures—despite the variety of products involved. Furthermore, moving from unit through process firms, there were increases in the length of line of command, the span of control of the chief executive, the proportion of wage costs to total costs, and in some personnel ratios. In the case of some other variables the relationship was curvilinear; that is, it was low in the unit firms, high in the mass-production firms, and again low in the process firms. This curvilinear relationship held true also in the span of control of first-line supervision and the proportion of skilled workers to unskilled. Even more striking, in view of the fact that we are comparing firms producing such diverse products as clothing, furniture, machinery, baked goods, autos, and chemicals, the most successful firms were those closest to the mean of their respective groups in such variables. If the mean for process firms was high on a particular variable, process firms registering still higher or below this mean did not do as well as those close to the group's mean.

After examining the kinds of conflicts and problems of the three types of firms, Woodward concluded that organizations have a dual function—technical, concerned with coordinating work and identifying authority, for example; and social, concerned with means of relating people so that they might work together. Similar distinctions are commonplace in organizational theory; for example, between formal and informal groups or processes, efficiency and effectiveness, production and tension management. But the value of Woodward's work is not specifically the distinction between technical and social functions, but her ability to use it as a variable—as something that legitimately *varies with organizations*. Thus, in processing firms, the technical function is more or less built into the design of the plant itself; management is free to devote a high proportion of its efforts to the social function. Furthermore, since the first function is accomplished so well, failure to do a good job in the second is not too important; techniques of handling the social function can vary greatly without too much effect upon organizational success.

In the unit firms, however, there is nothing automatic about the way the technical function must be performed. Therefore both technical and social functioning become quite important. But the unit firm can fairly easily mesh the two because the need for and degree of group independence are obvious—employees work together on one product at one work station. Furthermore, a short time cycle is involved, so that the importance of meshing the two functions is clear.

In mass-production firms (that is, large-batch, assembly, and mass production) the two functions inevitably conflict. Group independence is not visible, and the time cycles are very long. It is not possible to fuse line and staff roles or to concentrate on the network of relationships that enable people to work together. The technical and the social functions must evolve independently and piecemeal, since to rationalize production in such firms requires a high degree of specialization by humans, whereas in process firms, for example, the specialization is handled by equipment. Hence, Woodward finds the highest degree of conflict in the mass-production category. For example, such organizations had the most elaborate production-control procedures and the most rigorous sanctions. Production control in the process firms was no problem; it was primarily built into the manufacturing processes themselves. Production control in the unit firms was so difficult, however, the few firms were prepared to try to institute sophisticated controls and to predict results; these matters were left to the experience and know-how of the line supervisors.

Woodward's work also illuminates a problem that is frequently discussed in organizations: which functional group is the most important? For example, sales managers often say: "If you can't sell it, there is no use making it; sales must always have the final say; it is the customer who ultimately determines the success of our business." From the head of production one hears: "If you can't make it, everything stops right there; in the end, we are the most important." From research and development comes the claim: "You must have something that works better or lasts longer or does more than the other fellow's product; if you don't have it, there is not much use in making the same old thing and dumping it on the market."

Who is right? Drawing upon Woodward's scheme, we would say that the answer depends upon the technology of the production system. In unit and small-batch firms the cycle goes from marketing (finding a customer) to development (getting something to satisfy him) to production. There, development is the most critical; with a superior product, there is little trouble either producing it or finding customers, because custom items or small batches or prototypes are being made.

In large-batch and mass systems the cycle starts with development, for here there is large investment in inflexible resources necessitating long-range planning. But the critical phase is production, for here is where all-important cost reductions become possible and scheduling may be perfected for mass-assembly production or large batches. Marketing comes last—disposing of the product. The need for the product is well known since large-batch or mass production does not occur without high volume; the competitive edge is based upon price and delivery.

In process production, too, development comes first, but in this instance development involves more basic research to create new markets. Next comes marketing. Note that here marketing is not the last phase in the cycle. Mass markets of large volume must be created and assured before production can even begin because the inflexibility of process production is so great. Such items as new chemicals or processed foods developed by the laboratories must be test marketed or tried by other industrial consumers or packagers. In this way a market is assured; only then can production be undertaken. Of course, production facilities may not be easy to establish but, in contrast to the mass category, once underway these facilities are expected to run for a number of years with little trouble and little change.

Thus, we have seen that the critical function is different for each type of organization. Unit firms tend to be dominated by engineering personnel; mass-production firms by production people; process firms by marketers. Similarly, the relationships between these groups, the amounts and kinds of stresses, the difficulties of integration and cooperation vary in rather complex ways in each type. But the most important conclusion is that there is no evidence to prove that sales, production, or development is most important in all organizations. The importance of a function depends upon the specific technology employed.

With a comparative perspective like this, which shows that there is no "one best way" of doing things in all organizations, many well-accepted and even commonplace generalizations are challenged. Instead of applying to all or most cases, such generalizations hold true only for specific types, as we have just seen in terms of the importance of sales or production. To take another example, it is a venerable and generally unchallenged observation that to foster cooperation among groups it is necessary to bring them into close working contact. Often this is what is meant by "better communication" or "breaking down walls." According to Woodward, this gambit has been periodically attempted in the mass-production category, and it has generally failed. In fact, in cases where the design of the shops was such as to force the interaction of different groups, such as production and research, Woodward found relationships to be the poorest. However, in the unit and process categories, no particular effort was required to bring people together; interaction was built into the technology. Conflict was low in these cases. Thus, it might be wise to reduce communication or to build a few walls in certain kinds of technological systems.

Even those hoary platitudes about good personal relationships and close identification of people with the goals of the company fell by the wayside in the Woodward study. It was certainly not true, she says, that good relationships and close identification between the staff and the company had any clear correlation with success. They could be detrimental in a highly successful mass-production firm and seemed to be irrelevant to performance in process firms.

Only when we began to look at the differences between organizations and to categorize them in some meaningful way, such as by technology (though there are undoubtedly other ways), can we begin selectively to apply the multitude of insights offered by organizational analysis. These insights are both good and useful. Nevertheless, they have been, by and large, derived from studying one organization or a few similar organizations. They cannot be expected to apply to all organizations, unless they are so obvious and general as to be of limited utility. Joan Woodward, almost accidentally stumbling upon the idea of the technology of production systems (only those with their feet on the ground, ready to look closely at a threatening obstacle, ever "accidentally stumble" on something) has led the way for a number of researchers.

Summary

We began this chapter by giving a number of reasons why organizations become cluttered with rules, specialists, staff positions, restrictive procedures, and the like—all of which make them difficult to live with, slow to change, inflexible, and undemocratic. These aspects of structure were held to be necessary because of the need for specialization and for control over the non-organizational aspects of personnel, and the need to stabilize the effects of a changing environment. Large, complex organizations are necessarily imperfect tools. Men differ in their abilities, and they are neither perfect nor supermen. They are not machines created by and for the organization, but have their own goals, personalities, and interests outside the organization. The environment is never stable and predictable; means of coping with it must be developed. The solutions to such problems as hierarchies of authority, rules, and specialization carry their own costs. While these solutions are frequently criticized by those within and without the organization, no alternative way has been found to cope with the problem of organizing large numbers of people to produce goods and services efficiently.

However, the degree of bureaucratization does vary among organizations. Some organizations are willing to pay the price of high unit costs and to forego some of the economies of specialization and standardization. They do so because so little is known about designing, producing, and distributing the product that they have no choice; or because the environment is highly unstable; or because there is a demand for customized, high-quality goods. These organizations are less structured —or less bureaucratic—because they lack the characteristics that would make bureaucratization efficient.

We argued that the best way to conceive of these two types of organizations was in terms of their technology, which may be either routine or nonroutine. If the technology can be made routine (because of sufficient knowledge about designing, producing, and marketing goods and services and because there is a large enough market to permit volume production), then a high degree of structure or bureaucratization is possible and is efficient. If the technology is not routine, then the organization must forego the advantages of high volume production and clear and elaborate structure; it will be less bureaucratic.

However, we noted that in most organizations some units will be routine and others nonroutine. Thus, problems arise in the coordination of diverse units. We examined some of the ways of reducing the strains occasioned by a high degree of differentiation, in order to achieve the necessary integration.

We then examined more closely the concepts of routineness and nonroutineness, and we found that at least two different factors are involved: the degree of variability and the degree to which search behavior is analyzable. While routine organizations have little variability and invite analyzable search methods and nonroutine organizations have high variability and unanalyzable search methods, we argued that "craft" organizations are low on variability but have unanalyzable search methods, while "engineering" organizations are high on variability but utilize analyzable search methods. This analysis made it possible to divide organizations into four types, based upon their technology, and allowed us to make some complex predictions regarding the structure of these organizations. We also argued that some organizations which fail to match technology and structure in such matters as personnel assignment, organization, and control thereby run into trouble.

A somewhat different attempt to classify firms in terms of their technologies yielded three types: unit and small-batch production, large-batch and mass production, and continuous processing. A study based upon interviews and observations in a large number of firms so classified yielded a variety of valuable observations regarding the varying problems and competencies of the three types of firms.

But the main point stressed in the chapter is not whether there are three or four or more types of firms, or how technology is conceptualized or measured, but that firms differ according to the kind of work they do, and thus differ in their structure. Once this is realized, it becomes possible *selectively* to utilize the many techniques offered for solving organizational problems. By moving far beyond the simple, obvious differences between organizations such as Dick and Inland and the rayon mill and the electronics firm, discussed in the last chapter, to more complex models based upon analytic concepts such as raw materials and types of technologies, we are in a position to define more carefully the nature of any one organization and to see just what kind of management practices are likely to work and what kind are likely to fail.

chapter
four
The Environment

In Chapter One we appealed for a structural analysis of organizational phenomena, especially leadership. In Chapter Two we stressed the variety of types of organizations and the need to take account of this multiplicity. In Chapter Three we considered ways in which the variety of organizations might be conceptualized; first, simply as bureaucratic and nonbureaucratic, and then with progressively more complicated analytical schemes. But still we have explored only a portion of the sociological viewpoint in organizational analysis. We have omitted many organizational phenomena in which the sociologist, in particular, is interested. In the next two chapters, we will see that the organization is shaped by its environment. Over a period of time an organization changes in ways that can be roughly conceptualized and explained. It is a product of a "natural" history and unplanned changes. And finally it has goals which go beyond those officially stated in organizational handouts and charters.

At this point, we will make a distinct break with the preoccupations of the first three chapters. Earlier, we were primarily concerned with the internal analysis of organizational structure and functioning. Now, in this chapter, we will consider the environment of organizations; the nature of organizational goals will be scrutinized in the next chapter. Neither of these two general topics has been as well studied or conceptualized as organizational structure and behavior. So these chapters will be far more diffuse and anecdotal than the last three. No overall theory, such as the influence of technology on structure, can be used, and therefore the best approach is merely to consider topics in turn in some reasonable fashion. Nevertheless, the importance of the environment and goals is enormous. Furthermore, though our illustrations and discussions may lack theoretical guidance, they will certainly not lack interest and drama. Not all the action comes from within the organization.

Introduction

The Sociological Perspective: Background and Context

At the end of Chapter One we explored some aspects of the sociological craft in connection with the study of social structure. It is now appropriate to examine the role of the sociologist in another respect: his concern with the background and context of familiar behavior. The sociologist is often in the unique position of having a license to poach on the grounds of other disciplines. He considers the "sociological" aspects of phenomena that the political scientist, economist, psychologist, business school, or social-work school professor claims as his territory. He examines the "non-X" aspects of "X" behavior—the nonpolitical aspects of political behavior, for example. Whereas the conventional political scientist stresses constitutions, legislation, the formal structure of government, the formal aspects of elections and their outcome, the sociologist is likely to examine ethnicity, social class, interpersonal relations, and economic institutions in his analysis of political behavior. He asks, how do these "nonpolitical" factors influence political behavior? When the sociologist examines economic behavior he again emphasizes the "noneconomic" aspects, such as social stratification, group influences, and cultural norms.

In the case of organizational analysis, the sociologist tends to play down the official and formal aspects of organizations, which have been considered by those concerned with business administration, public administration, operations research, and human engineering. Instead, he has been prone to emphasize informal group relations and the informal structure of organizations, as well as the role of extra-organizational influences upon personnel, such as racial or ethnic origin, attitudes towards authority, and career perspectives. Of course, he also considers the environment in which the organization exists. It is as if the sociologist were studying the "underlife" and the "overlife" of the organization—those contextual aspects not readily visible and without obvious relevance.

One handicap is associated with this perspective and, indeed, with the sociological enterprise in general. Unfortunately, every reader is his own sociologist. In contrast to many other disciplines that tell the reader about a technical area with which he is not too familiar, the sociologist describes a world that is familiar to all. Thus, much of his description appears to be "obvious." The rub is that we all carry around in ourselves contradictory explanations, each of which seems equally obvious; we bring out the one which suits us at the time.

It is "obvious," for example, that an individual will be happier with his job when he has a good deal of discretion than he would be if he has little discretion. Although this conclusion seems obvious, we cannot be positive; therefore we must make a number of studies to prove the obvious. Then it will develop that the truism is not always true, and the equally obvious alternative will be demonstrated—it will appear that job satisfaction goes with discretion only in certain situations, for if a worker comes from an environment or background that does not place a high value on discretion (and many do not), or if discretion creates too many tensions, or if a worker does not want to be so much involved in his work (and probably does not have to be) then satisfaction declines with the addition of discretion. Is not this an obvious conclusion? But the opposite was equally obvious. In many situations an obvious case can be made on either side. Then the social scientist (and especially, apparently, the sociologist) is left with the melancholy assignment of proving one case, rather than the other, and he must face being told that his conclusions were obvious all along. Or, he has the task of specifying the exact conditions under which one obvious relationship will hold, and the conditions under which an equally obvious but quite different relationship will hold.

The sociologist also has the dreary job of calling attention to facts which we take for granted (and which are thus too obvious or common to bother with) and of utilizing these commonplaces in the analysis of social life. In the United States we take for granted a whole set of cultural conditions which permit the efficient functioning of complex organizations—such as literacy, authority relations, and an emphasis upon achievement as a basis of judging people rather than characteristics ascribed at birth. But it is a mistake to take these conditions for granted, for they explain a good deal about our society and its organizations. Consider, for example, the wholly recondite, familiar, and even trivial matter of time.

Time and the Organization

Probably nothing is as obvious as the fact that organizational behavior is precisely timed—for example, people can be counted on to come to work at a certain time and leave at a certain time, year in and year out; documents are given dates; appointments can be made and kept; productivity can be measured in terms of time, and thus labor costs calculated. But once such an obvious "non-organizational" characteristic is considered seriously, time becomes a problematical variable that serves a useful purpose. Welfare agencies are run on a schedule that may be convenient to the employees, but often quite inconvenient to the clients who are supposed to be served. Hospital operating rooms, with their enormous capital investment and their crowded schedules, are idle in the afternoons and nights because of the time customs of doctors. Factories in underdeveloped areas (including some parts of the southern United States) sometimes must make a great effort to "socialize," as we say, employees to the importance of an unvarying time schedule; people accustomed to rural occupations have a flexible time schedule, based on nature's clock. Industrial engineers sometimes sacrifice sensible work procedures and introduce cumbersome artifices so that productivity on individual items and jobs can be precisely calculated in terms of units of time.

Status in organizations is correlated with freedom from the clock or discretion in the use of time. The time span of review of performance increases steadily as one mounts the organizational ladder; this span has even been used as a measure of rank and equitable salary (31). One of the most moving and fascinating essays in industrial sociology is called "Of Time and the Railroader" (12). It discusses the effect upon human relationships of round-the-clock operations on a precise time schedule. Not to belabor the point, an obvious cultural factor—conceptions and uses of time—can become a useful tool for stating or analyzing a problem.

The Grand Schemes

We will not detail the various grand theoretical schemes which relate the rise of large-scale organizations, and particularly capitalism, to massive changes in environment, culture, social structure, technology, political systems, nation-states. However, two such schemes deserve brief mention. Max Weber, a sociologist writing in Germany in the first decade of this century, sought to account for both the emergence of the bureaucratic form of administration in all large organizations and the rise of capitalism (88, 90). He traced these developments to such factors as a money economy, mobile labor supply, the emergence of the centralized nation-state, and the ethics of Protestantism, especially the Calvinist sects.

Joseph Schumpeter, the economic historian, writing in the 1940s, focused upon capitalism itself, and related it to the social structure which provided an upper stratum of persons with political power who could protect the emergent capitalists and a middle stratum who could provide the mass support needed in democratic nations (66). But he foresaw that the spirit of entrepreneurship would give way to managerial capitalism and that the economic process, by stripping away the power of old institutions and beliefs, would undermine the support for capitalism itself. Intellectuals, leading the disaffected elements of the middle class and the working class, would launch an attack which would eventually "socialize" the system; innovation would be routinized, myths would be destroyed, aspirations of the lower classes would rise astronomically, and the managers would have neither the incentives nor the fortitude to protect the system.

Both men viewed large organizations as being born of changing social and cultural conditions, and as, in turn, changing these very conditions as they grew larger. Organizations influence their environment, as well as being influenced by it, once they become large, powerful, and indispensable. Both men looked upon the future with a detached, scholarly horror, as they saw this tool that man had invented get out of control and continue to influence man and society through its own inexorable logic. Their concern is echoed today in the cries of the radical right for reduced governmental power and the autonomy of the individual, the cries of the radical left for exactly the same things, and in the feverish attempts of some social scientists to democratize, decentralize, and humanize our large organizations. The large organization has become the environment for man and society in terms of these broad, long-range perspectives. Reorganization, responsiveness, and regulation have become the preoccupations of those who see the threat to industrial societies posed by large organizations.

Outline of the Chapter

In this chapter we shall restrict ourselves to less global aspects of organization-environment relationships. The topics we shall consider are those which provide more specific insights into the working of particular types of organizations and more specific awareness of matters of which the manager does well to be aware. First we shall examine the question of organizational legitimacy. It is generally assumed that an organization has a protected status in society as long as its output is considered legitimate. Yet many organizations find, often to their surprise, that sectors of the public question their goods and services and seek to restrict or withdraw this protected status. On the other hand, some organizations find themselves in the position of being required to provide certain goods and services, and only with difficulty can they withdraw from certain activities. The executive had better be aware of the grounds of legitimacy for his organization and the very real possibility that they may shift without his being prepared for the ensuing crisis.

One way to insure legitimacy is to bring into the organization those groups who would threaten its stability—a process called "cooptation." We will examine some examples of this strategy. We will also consider the more general problem that arises when organizational members have vested interests in other organizations and these outside influences must be controlled. The successful organization knows not only how to neutralize sectors of its environment, but also how to utilize them.

The regional or cultural setting of an organization also affects its performance. This factor will be touched upon in terms of the characteristics of the work force, where matters such as strikes, morale, and productivity may have little to do with specific efforts of managers but a great deal to do with the background and social life of the employees.

The impact of cultural differences is greater, of course, when firms move out of the United States and establish branches abroad. The subject of multinational organizations, or those operating in foreign cultures, is too broad to deal with here, but some remarks about one particularly acute problem are illustrative—the American executive and his family abroad. We take for granted so many of our cultural and social props; this example allows us to be aware of just how heavily we depend upon our environment.

Finally, in broadly considering the environment we will describe some instances when cultural beliefs prevented the introduction of laborsaving devices and inspection procedures; these examples involve the seemingly unlikely use of pigeons as workers.

To any organization, the most important segment of the environment is other organizations, particularly organizations of competitors and customers. In order to minimize the uncertainties in this area, and to maximize profitability, organizations have developed a number of devices. One of these is reciprocity—"you scratch my back and I'll scratch yours." Another is the informal and pervasive suspension of competition, or at least its mitigation. What is meant here is not price fixing or cartels so much as informal practices of mutual benefit among supposed enemies.

Finally, we shall touch upon the matter of business and politics. Business is in, and has always been in, politics, both directly through donations and manpower and indirectly by doing or refusing to take actions which affect the distribution of political power in communities and the nation. As already noted, the environment does not merely impinge upon organizations. Organizations, as we shall see in the discussion of business and politics, are the environment for other organizations and groups in society.

Legitimizing the Organization

Talcott Parsons (52) has raised the question of legitimacy with respect to organizations in society, a seemingly obvious matter we are likely to take for granted. He argues that in any social system the output of one aspect of that system will be consumed by other aspects of the system and thus this output must be desired and therefore legitimized. Legitimization comes from such groups as consumers, suppliers, regulatory agencies, the investigating public, and taxpayers—all part of the organization's environment. One of the implicit tasks of an organization, then, is to establish the legitimacy of its output (and, we might add, the legitimacy of its method of operation). In the economic sector it is generally thought that this end is achieved through market mechanisms. That is, if an organization produces something that somebody else wants, the purchase itself confers legitimacy upon the organization and its output. Prostitution, organized crime, and the numbers racket, to cite only a few such enterprises, are not exceptions. If no one can be persuaded to buy its product the organization will not survive; "illegitimate" organizations not only survive but prosper.

Actually, it is not quite so simple to achieve legitimacy. Many economic organizations spend a great deal of their resources to convince potential customers of the legitimacy of their output—that is, that people should buy it, that they need it, and that they lose status by not having it. Some organizations face extreme challenges. For example, the tobacco industry has proclaimed through its spokesmen that if it were absolutely proven that smoking tobacco causes cancer they would stop making cigarettes. Cigarettes would not be a legitimate output. Of course, what the tobacco industry means by absolute proof is quite different from what the U.S. Department of Health, Education, and Welfare, the Surgeon General's Office, or the American Cancer Society means by proof. On almost any scale a titanic battle is being waged to certify the legitimacy of this output. The auto industry, too, has periodically been questioned as to the legitimacy of producing mobile weapons which are "unnecessarily" lethal—in terms of such features as their enormous power, speed, impaling devices on front grills and dash boards, and safety hazards related to tires, brakes, and aerodynamic stability.

Legitimacy for nonprofit organizations is sometimes an even greater problem. Government agencies die more frequently than we realize because their legitimacy is questioned, and other agencies expend great resources to stay alive. Often this is merely a matter of another organization incorporating the market of the organization under attack, as in the deadly serious warfare between the Army and the Air Force over who should provide air cover for ground troops. But in other cases, as in the demise of the Farm Security Administration in the 1940s, the issue is legitimacy. In this instance, a depression-born organization attempting to serve poor farmers was eradicated by powerful interests in the Agriculture Department who represented wealthy farmers in the Grange and the Farm Bureau Federation. The Office of Economic Opportunity—the major weapon in the "war on poverty" in the 1960s—is, at this writing, having its legitimacy questioned by those who would transfer its operations to the less controversial, more cumbersome, and generally ineffective federal Welfare and Labor departments. Of course, the very creation of OEO signified at least a temporary crisis in legitimacy for existing organizations concerned with welfare, jobs, and health. The rise and fall of organizations, governmental and nongovernmental, is a sensitive barometer of the social and political problems of our society. They are born and die in larger numbers than most people realize, since we are usually aware only of those which survive for long periods.

The executive (even, for example, the head of giant General Motors, which is supposedly under constant surveillance by a tiny segment of the Justice Department, which would like to break it up) can never take the legitimacy of his organization completely for granted. Survival—presumably a constant preoccupation of almost all organizations—depends not only on such mundane matters as efficiency and profits, but upon the acceptance of output and methods of operation by significant sectors of the organization's environment. A few years ago large prestigious universities had not yet experienced crises of legitimacy. Today, most of them are attacked, on the one hand, by radical students who deny the legitimacy of the university as it is now constituted and, on the other hand, by conservative legislators and voters who deny the legitimacy of those segments of university operation which seem to provide a haven for radical ideologies. Many a university president has had occasion to intone the somber warning: "The very existence of this institution is at stake."

A nice reverse twist on the legitimacy aspect of environmental relationships concerns the elimination of legitimate output, or the refusal to engage in legitimate output. Thus, the railroad industry has sought for at least 30 years to close down many lines which the operators claim are unprofitable. The railroad commission has consistently opposed a small percentage of these requests on the grounds that service must be provided, and the railroad cannot go out of this particular business. Bus lines in cities are a similar example. Again, some state land-grant universities would prefer to reduce the size of their agricultural schools, in view of greater needs in other areas, but cannot do so because of the strength of farming interests. We will return in a moment to the question of the elimination of legitimate output.

The issue of legitimacy in economic organizations is closely involved with good corporate citizenship or responsible professional management. Rarely does the problem concern a single illegitimate output, as in the tobacco industry. Generally the question revolves about a few presumably illegitimate products among many legitimate ones. When the drug industry is charged with distributing and selling some drugs which they know to be potentially harmful or probably worthless, it is recognized that this is only a part of their legitimate and worthwhile output.

The social mechanisms for assessing the legitimacy of an output are quite clumsy. The thalidomide case breathed new life into Senator Kefauver's investigations of the drug industry and resulted in some significant disclosures and some mild legislation (27, 49). But it was an accident that the case erupted at that particular time and was so well publicized. The inept efforts of General Motors Corporation to discredit author Ralph Nader, and thus his book on irresponsibility in the auto industry (50), significantly increased the impact of that book and abetted the congressional investigation that resulted in some new safety features. But that was a clumsy accident on the part of General Motors.

By and large, we resign ourselves to relying upon the market mechanism and on the phrase, "let the buyer beware," to judge legitimacy. The market mechanism, of course, is significantly influenced by heavy advertising expenditures, collusion, and other extraneous factors. The public might be willing to pay for good inexpensive housing rather than to buy plastic baubles if the opportunity to purchase inexpensive housing were available. By and large, we really rely upon the good conscience of the powerful people who run and direct large corporations, to maintain an adequate level of legitimacy in economic outputs.

In this respect the following article by Blair Ewing, a political scientist, is most instructive. Again, this is a case of legitimacy in reverse. Can a corporation legitimately withdraw a desired product from the public? Mr. Ewing states the issue otherwise, but I think that you will see the connection.

The Good Goldfish: A Case Study in the Corporate Conscience

A host of respectable men have lately informed the American public that it labors under a misconception about business and businessmen. The greedy, selfish, entrepreneur with his "public be damned" point of view is no longer with us, the upright men tell us. "The tycoon is dead," *Fortune* magazine tells us in an advertisement. This nasty old capitalist has been replaced by the new corporate manager, with his new corporate conscience, his sense of public responsibility, and his foremost desire to serve the public good while serving also his board, his stockholders, and his customers.

This model of civic excellence is the subject of praise or analysis or both by such impressive academic, government, and business figures as Frederick Lewis Allen, Adolf A. Berle, Jr., Russell Davenport, David Lilienthal, John Kenneth Galbraith, Talcott Parsons, Peter Drucker, and John W. Hill. They differ as to whether the new businessmen can help being motivated by the demands of the public for social responsibility on the part of business; but none of them deny that his actions are guided by considerations of public welfare.

Frederick Lewis Allen tells us, for example, that new style corporate management "must always steer its course with an eye to how its actions will look, not only to its employees, its stockholders, its customers, and the government, but also to the general public." Public scrutiny, says Allen, has left businesses and businessmen "with about as much sense of privacy as a goldfish." And, he adds: "A goldfish has got to be good."[1]

Much more explicit about the nature of our "good gold-fish" businessman and the considerations which guide his activities is Adolf A. Berle, Jr. One of the major limits to economic power, according to Berle, is the public consensus, which produces corporate social responsibility. Of this limitation, he says that it is "intangible, imponderable in character, but wholly real." Further, it is a mistake to ridicule this limitation by referring to it sneeringly as "the corporate conscience," he says. It is a "reality," and violation of the limits it imposes "leads to loss of prestige, public standing, and popular esteem for the men in the organization itself." Further, "if loss of prestige does not produce results more acceptable to the community, other and more forceful means of imposing the ideas embodied in the public consensus . . . commonly appear." Berle completes his remarks on the subject by giving us a fairly precise definition of the new corporate conscience. It is "a set of ideas, widely held by the community, and often by the organization itself and the men who direct it, that certain uses are 'wrong,' that is, contrary to the established interest and value system of the community."[2]

The evidence piles higher. Russell Davenport and the editors of Fortune tell us that "the manager is becoming a professional in the sense that like all professional men he has a responsibility to society as a whole" and "is part of a group that enjoys power only so long as it does not abuse it."[3] The old concept that the owner could do as he pleased with his property has been replaced, Davenport et al. declare, by "the belief that ownership carries social obligations, and that a manager is a trustee not only for the owner, but for society as a whole."[4]

David Lilienthal joins the chorus. "Our top industrial

[1] Frederick Lewis Allen, The Big Change (New York: Pennant Books, 1952), pp. 187–188.
[2] Adolf A. Berle, Jr., Power without Property (New York: Harcourt, Brace & World, Inc., 1959), p. 90.
[3] Russell Davenport and the editors of Fortune, U.S.A.: The Permanent Revolution (New York: Prentice-Hall, Inc., 1951), pp. 79–80.
[4] Ibid., p. 88.

leadership has assumed, and it now bears, not only responsibility for production itself, but for a whole range of the
social and political problems which are to be found in a
modern industrialized nation. In short, there has been a revolution in the nature of active responsibility of Big Business.
The president of a large company is now responsible to prac-
tically everybody!"[5]

That distinguished debunker of "conventional wisdom," John Kenneth Galbraith, tells us that whether the
businessman wishes it or not, his actions are guided and controlled by considerations of social responsibility. He says that,
"dogmatically stated . . . private economic power is held
in check by the countervailing power of those who are subject to it. The first begets the second."[6] He does allow for
exceptions, but he calls this "a common rule."[7]

Still another distinguished social theorist, Talcott Parsons, tells us that the common notion that business is guided
solely by self-interest and that by contrast the professions
are guided only by altruism is wrong. Both business and the
professions are guided by both principles. As Parsons puts it,
"the whole occupational sphere is dominated by a single
fundamental goal, that of 'success.' The content of this common goal will, of course, vary with the specific character of
the functional role. But whatever this may be, it will involve both interested and disinterested elements. On the
disinterested side will be above all two components, a disinterested devotion to 'good work' . . . and a disinterested
acceptance of the moral patterns which govern this activity
with respect to such matters as respecting the rights of
others."[8]

Still another statement of management's public responsibility comes from Peter Drucker, who tells us that: "It is
management's responsibility to *make* whatever is genuinely
in the public good *become* the enterprise's own self-inter-

[5] David Lilienthal, *Big Business: A New Era* (New York: Harper & Row,
Publishers, Inc., 1952), p. 30.

[6] John Kenneth Galbraith, *American Capitalism*, 2nd ed. (Boston: Houghton Mifflin Company, 1956), p. 111.

[7] *Ibid.*, p. 113.

[8] Talcott Parsons, "The Motivation of Economic Activities," in Talcott
Parsons, *Essays in Sociological Theory* (New York: Free Press of Glencoe, 1949),
pp. 212–214.

est."⁹ Even more explicitly, Drucker declares that "there is a responsibility of management to the public interest as such. This is based on the fact that the enterprise is an organ of society."¹⁰

Finally, public relations man John W. Hill tells us quite simply that "the purpose of a commercial corporation is to serve the needs or wants of people."¹¹

The assertions that this "good goldfish" businessman exists and is typical are plentiful and impressive, not only because of the eloquence and fervor with which they are stated, but also because of the sources from which they come.

But a problem nags. The theorists give us little in the way of concrete examples of the new businessman in action. If we want to discover such a man, where should we turn? If we assume that this business community is generally possessed of this new corporate conscience, then we may also assume that those whom the business community honors for outstanding achievement will possess the corporate conscience in its most perfect form, will be the best of all goldfish. Among those honored by the business community, we should be able to find a case study in the corporate conscience, in the social responsibility of the new style businessman.

Such a man is J. Patrick Lannan, who was honored in the spring of 1962 with the Chicago Association of Commerce and Industry's Horatio Alger Award, an award given a Chicago businessman who has risen from poverty to riches and has made an "outstanding contribution" to American business and American life. If the theorists are right, and if our assumptions based on their assertions are correct, then J. Patrick Lannan ought to be our real-life good goldfish.

What sort of man, then, is J. Patrick Lannan? First, he is a self-made man, a high school drop-out who made good, a one-time machinist who in 1962 at the age of 57 was a millionaire. Secondly, he has had a long and highly successful career as an insurance broker, investment banker, publisher, railroad owner, mining and oil executive. Finally,

⁹ Peter Drucker, *The Practice of Management* (New York: Harper & Row, Publishers, Inc., 1954), p. 390.
¹⁰ *Ibid.*, p. 386.
¹¹ John W. Hill, *Corporate Public Relations: Arm of Modern Management* (New York: Harper & Row, Publishers, Inc., 1958).

he is a director of more than a score of prosperous companies. None of this seems by itself to set him apart from others whose achievements are similar. Wherein lies his *real* distinction, and the presumed reason for his special award?

Perhaps it is in the fact that he has been very largely responsible for the demise of two enterprises, one of which served a reading public of over four million, the other of which served a riding public of nearly five million. And the deaths of those enterprises came despite public demand for continuation of them. This is distinction, this is Mr. Lannan's claim to difference. This is perhaps why he has been marked out for special attention by his fellow businessmen.

The case of the riders is more recent, more fascinating and more distinctive, and therefore it might be best to look first at it. What Lannan did, in brief was to force a commuter railroad, the Chicago, North Shore and Milwaukee, which he controlled through a holding company, out of business as of January 21, 1963. This 106-mile, electric-powered road served the populous Lake Michigan shore area between Chicago and Milwaukee, which, according to the 1960 census, is the fastest growing part of the Chicago metropolitan area. The road carried until 1961 around five million passengers annually, or about 12,000 a day, though the figures for 1962 were closer to four million and 10,000.

Aside from the serious immediate effects on these commuters and on the road's 700 employes, the ultimate effect of the abandonment of the line has been to pour millions of dollars into the treasury of a railroad holding company, the Lannan-controlled Susquehanna Corporation. This seems a curious outcome, at first glance. One has always thought that in the normal course of events business avoided losing more money by going out of business, but made money by staying in business. But Lannan has managed a magnificent maneuver through which he will make money by destroying one of the enterprises he has controlled.

The story of Lannan's North Shore (the short name for the railroad) coup begins in 1953, when the Illinois Commerce Commission, the state body which regulates railroads, approved a reorganization of the North Shore on the understanding that the road, which had not been making money since the boom days of World War II, would continue to operate.

Five million dollars in cash and other assets were removed from the railroad in the course of reorganization and
used to establish, first, a subsidiary company, and then in
further reorganization a parent company, now called the
Susquehanna Corporation. Susquehanna became full owner
of the subsidiary railroad operating company and used the
$5 million in rail assets to build—in less than a decade—a $9
million investment in uranium mills, phosphate, sulfuric
acid, computer plants, shale deposits, and bus companies,
all of them mostly in the West. Susquehanna earned a net
of over $2 million in 1959 and had pre-tax earnings of about
$2 million in 1960. But not a penny of the $5 million was
returned to the railroad, and only a few thousand dollars of
Susquehanna profits had been spent for railroad purposes.
The parent company made several loans to the railroad, all
of them repayable.

With Susquehanna well-established and profitable by
1958, the road asked the Interstate Commerce Commission,
which has sole jurisdiction over such matters, for permission
to abandon the railroad. At hearings in every year since
1958 before the ICC and in federal courts in Chicago, where
the issue of abandonment was argued, the road claimed that
it had lost money and that its losses were steadily increasing.
It is true that the road lost money except during wartime. It
is further true that the road was in receivership from 1908
to 1916 and again from 1932 to 1946, but it is also true that
total losses from the beginning of 1946 to mid-1961 were
$5,778,296, a figure not much larger than the $5 million
removed from the railroad's books in 1953. The figures are
taken from documents submitted by the North Shore to the
Illinois Commerce Commission. Thus the question of
whether the road might have made a profit after 1953 cannot be satisfactorily answered. If the $5 million had been
used for improvements designed to make the road profitable,
it might have. But Susquehanna has foreclosed this question
by its actions.

When asked to comment early in 1961 on Susquehanna's removal of the assets in 1953, Lannan, who was then
and is now board chairman of Susquehanna, told a special
investigatory committee of the Illinois House of Representatives that the road had been and continued to be chronically
unprofitable. No amount of money could save the North
Shore, he assured the committee. The committee was not

impressed and in its report issued May 17, 1961, it called the abandonment effort "the final culmination of an undisclosed financial scheme," the purpose of which was, it asserted, "to destroy the railroad."

The committee, the Illinois Commerce Commission, and a group of riders organized as the North Shore Commuters Association referred to the following sequence of events as evidence of a long-term plan to abandon:

(1) In January, 1954, less than a year after reorganization, when it had promised to continue in operation, the Road asked the Illinois Commerce Commission for permission to abandon its Shore Line operation, a branch of the road running quite near Lake Michigan north of Chicago. Permission was granted in 1955.

(2) In 1954, Charles S. Leonard, a Chicago financial consultant, was retained by the North Shore to analyze the operations of the new holding company. He recommended that the railroad be abandoned at a later date when substantial tax losses generated would be of most advantage to the parent corporation.

(3) In April, 1958, this same Mr. Leonard was employed as president of the railroad.

(4) In June, 1958, the railroad asked the ICC to permit it to abandon its entire line.

(5) In the late fall of 1960, Susquehanna published an investment brochure designed to attract investors. It pointed out in the brochure that among its principal resources was the potential tax loss from abandonment of the railroad. It said this would be about $17 to $20 million, a figure it arrived at by subtracting the salvage value (estimated at about $8 million) from the book value (estimated at about $25 to $28 million). The book value is the value of the road as an operating property. The salvage value is the value of the property and rolling stock after abandonment. The brochure pointed out that the tax loss, under federal law, could be carried forward five years, backward four, and could be applied against the holding company's profits. The cash which would come from sale of the road as salvage was listed in the brochure as another attractive resource.

The brochure concluded by saying that "the important point to remember is that the disposition of the railroad will permit $25–$28 million of cash generation exclusive of depreciation, over the next several years, to be reemployed in the faster growing and more profitable phases of the company's business."

(6) During 1960, Susquehanna hired and paid a public relations firm to contact newspaper editors in the area served by the railroad and to try to convince them that the road should be permitted to abandon operations. This expenditure of Susquehanna funds for railroad purposes has been the only rail expense Susquehanna has been willing to bear.

(7) The railroad made no improvements on existing rolling stock and bought no new rolling stock during the period Lannan controlled the road's destinies. The newest equipment was bought in 1941, with 127 of the 135 cars more than 30 years old. With some of the $5 million taken from the road in 1953, new equipment might have been bought which might have helped the road compete more effectively for riders.

(8) Mr. Harold Mason, the road's president at the time of abandonment, admitted that the only advertising the road had done "in recent years" was to paint its name on its bridges and underpasses, to print timetables and to hang signs with its name on its stations.

(9) Lannan, besides being Susquehanna board chairman and a North Shore director, bought stock in and became a director and then more recently also chairman of the executive committee of another Chicago commuter road, the Chicago, Milwaukee, St. Paul and Pacific, which competes with the North Shore between Chicago and Milwaukee. Lannan also is a director of the Greyhound Corporation, which competed with both railroads for passengers, as does the Chicago and North Western, in the area north and northwest of Chicago. Interlocking directorates of this kind are permitted in transportation companies by the Interstate Commerce Commission, which gave Lannan permission for this arrangement. Both the Milwaukee Road and Greyhound are profitable operations, largely because their operations are diversified and extended over a large area, while the North

Shore is confined to the Chicago-Milwaukee area. Both the Milwaukee Road and Greyhound will no doubt make still more money now that the North Shore is out of the picture.

(10) Finally, the managements of the North Shore and the Milwaukee Road resisted efforts to solve the dilemma through public action. Both roads opposed efforts by the Chicago Transit Authority, the public body which operates buses, subways, and the elevated, and by Chicago's Mayor Richard Daley to obtain permission and to make a tax deal which would have made it possible for the CTA to buy the North Shore and operate at least that part of it in Illinois.

This whole series of steps and events indicates, I think it is fair to say, a fairly clear plan to abandon the road considerably before 1958, and perhaps as early as 1954, shortly after reorganization and a promise to continue operations. The whole course of events indicates further an outright disregard for the public interest and a flagrant disregard of the railroad's role as a regulated public utility operating under a certificate of public convenience and necessity. Such a certificate ought to mean something to the "new style" businessman.

The ICC was aware of the whole argument of the opponents of abandonment—and these included, besides the Illinois Commerce Commission, the North Shore Commuters Association, and the Illinois House legislative committee, the City of Milwaukee, the City of Chicago, and the State of Illinois (represented by its Attorney General, William Clark)—when it issued an interim order in the case in May, 1960. The order told the railroad to continue operations for a one-year trial period, explaining that: "It must be certain that everything possible has been done to operate the line at a profit and that its proposed abandonment was not merely a convenient method of securing tax reductions for the parent company, which would benefit to a far greater extent than it could hope to benefit from continuing service."

As to whether "everything possible" was done in that period, the argument is largely irrelevant. The railroad cut expenses, but not as much as the Illinois Commerce Commission said it could have. Rates were raised 23%, but the road also raised wages. In any case, as might have been predicted, the road continued to lose money in the interim period. As an interesting footnote to this problem of costs, one cost was the payment of insurance fees by the railroad to none other than Lannan & Co., insurance brokers, a company of which J. Patrick Lannan is president. Accident and fire insurance rates went up in 1961, the year during which Lannan hoped to get final abandonment, because of the poor condition of the road's equipment. Mr. Lannan doesn't miss a trick. He also is a director of Automatic Canteen Corporation of America, which has long held the concession for the automatic dispensing machines in all the North Shore stations.

Largely as a result of the showing of continued losses in riders and in revenues, the ICC finally issued an order on May 18, 1962, authorizing abandonment of the entire North Shore line, subject to the condition that the road should be sold to any responsible party for not less than the net salvage value. The North Shore Commuters Association attempted and failed to raise enough money through sale of stock to commuters and railroad employes to purchase and operate the road. And on January 21, 1963, the end of the line came for the North Shore.

It is the sort of exploit which would have struck that trio of nineteenth century railroad rapscallions, Fisk, Gould, and Drew, as worthy of—though more subtle than—some of their efforts. Lannan, of course, is well within the law. But the venture seems to have been informed by the self-same spirit which informed the actions of those earlier railroad manipulators: milk the railroad dry and the public be damned. Is this what a "good goldfish" is expected to do?

Everyone is familiar with the results of the decline of railroad commuter service. Accompanying it is a rise in traffic congestion in the large cities, an increasing number of enormously expensive expressways, a growth in the number of parking lots, a decline in the tax revenues of the city as the amount of taxable property declines because of increased use for automobiles and their needs. In short, if the trend continues, Chicago will become a copy of Los Angeles with regard to transportation.

Furthermore, a dangerous pattern may be set. Other railroad managements, equally possessed of corporate consciences, will be encouraged to imitate Lannan's success in closing down the North Shore. His example provides a convenient route for withdrawal from commuter service.

Let us now look into Mr. Lannan's other interesting

distinction, his role in the demise of *Colliers* six years ago, at a time when its circulation was almost 4.2 million. Hollis Alpert, in an article in the *Saturday Review* on May 11, 1957, describes Lannan's procedure.

Apparently some $4 million was invested in Crowell-Collier, the company which published *Colliers,* by Lannan and other Chicago investors associated with him. *Colliers* and *The American,* another Crowell-Collier publication, both were losing money, while the Crowell-Collier book publishing department was making money. Shortly after Lannan and friends were elected directors of the company, the suspension of both magazines was announced. Alpert points out that when a corporation consists of two parts, one profitable and one not, the stock of the company can be expected to sell at some sort of "median value." The strategy one might then be tempted to follow is to obtain control of the corporation and put the losing part of the business out of business. This, Alpert quite reasonably suggests, will lead to a rise in the price of the corporation's stock and a profit for the speculators.

Mr. Lannan's method now becomes clear. The design is as follows: Find a situation in which one business, or part of a business, is losing money, and another competing business or another part of the business is profitable. Then buy into the business or businesses involved, gaining control and, if necessary, reorganizing the company. Then abandon or dump the losing part of the business or the losing business. The results one can expect are that the stock of the surviving part of the company or the surviving company goes up. One may also realize tax write-offs, in certain cases. And the public, whether it be a reading or a riding public, or any other kind of public, be damned.

The strategy is an admirable one for making money, but those who follow it scarcely fit the image of the "good goldfish" businessman we have been told flourishes among us. What are we to conclude, in Mr. Lannan's case? Is the confidence of the business community misplaced? Is Mr. Lannan atypical and to be regarded as a kind of throwback to an earlier age, a breed if not extinct, then shortly to be so? Or could it even be that this new style is not so widely adopted and widely admired as we have been led to believe?

The theorists may not be wrong. But they have not demonstrated that the corporate conscience does exist. We

have no documentation from them to support their assertions. On the other hand, we have in the case of Lannan and
his admirers some concrete evidence that the reverse of what
Berle says is true; that, rather than "loss of prestige," there
is a gain in prestige for a man who demonstrated that his
corporation had *no* "corporate conscience." Given this state
of things, we are obliged to reject as without current foundation in fact the assertions of the theorists that the "corporate
conscience" is a real limit on corporate behavior.[12]

Mr. Ewing no doubt overstates the case when he says we are
obligated to reject the assertion that a corporate conscience exists and is
a limit on corporate behavior. It would not be difficult to document
many examples of such limitation. However, it is striking that, during
this period of publicized strife, Mr. Lannan was honored with the
Horatio Alger Award of the Chicago Association of Commerce and
Industry for having made an outstanding contribution to American
business and American life. Of such things is legitimacy compounded.

Thus, the seemingly commonplace observation of Parsons that an
organization's output must be legitimized by society—or the more
general point that organizations exist in an active and fluid environment—has led us to consider some of the more lively and interesting
controversies about economic and welfare organizations in the 1960s.
Most of our formal theories of organization take legitimacy for granted
—as do most organizations themselves. But both theory and practice do
so at their peril. In a time of rapid social change and rising social
criticism, the legitimacy of organizations in every sector of our society
has been questioned, and the questioning has begun to expose the
elaborate methods used by some organizations to forestall inquiry, divert
attention, or to create legitimacy for questionable operations. The social
sciences have done little to investigate this area of interface between the
organization and the public.

Neutralizing and Utilizing the Environment

The environment is always both a threat and a resource. Sometimes it is clearly one or the other, and at other times what might have
been a threat can be made over into a resource—at a cost, of course. The

---

[12] Blair Ewing, *The Good Goldfish: A Case Study in the Corporate Conscience.* Reprinted with permission of the author.

mechanisms for dealing with the environment of competing organizations have been examined in general terms by James Thompson.[13] But the most detailed examination comes from a case study of the Tennessee Valley Authority by Philip Selznick (68), in which costs and strategies of dealing with a complex political and economic environment are detailed. The TVA was engaged in generating electrical power, producing fertilizer and flood control, but Selznick did not consider these aspects directly. Rather, he deals with the following activities, which stemmed from the basic functions: distributing fertilizer to farmers, improving crop-production facilities, organizing rural electrical cooperatives, handling the displacement of people caused by the building of large dams which flooded valuable bottom farming land, utilizing the land around the large lakes either for community recreational use or for development by private entrepreneurs, and, finally, conservation work, particularly in connection with logging and forestry.

Selznick found that in order to neutralize congressional opposition to the TVA—this was in the 1930s, when the agency was criticized as being socialistic and unfairly competitive with private enterprise—the Authority had to make certain critical bargains at the grass-roots level. As a result, the reclamation and social programs were handled in such a way that local power interests were not alienated. This meant that "county courthouse" politics permeated programs related to service, free fertilizer, access to waterfront land, and the relocation programs, among others. The programs were administered in such a way as to favor the whites and the more wealthy farmers, at the expense of the poor and Negro farmers. This was done by bringing into the TVA, as staff members, representatives of the "vested" interests in the area—the land-grant college system, the county-agent system, and the Farm Bureau Federation. Representatives of these interests soon controlled most of the programs administered by this part of TVA; in return, congressional opposition to the TVA was presumably minimized. However, the cost of this accommodation was high for the poor farmers in the area and for those who wished to preserve forests and public recreational areas. Selznick labeled the process as one of cooptation: to minimize a threat from the environment the organization coopts or brings into the organization leaders from the environment who then will have some say in the organization's policies. This proved to be a controversial technique in

---

[13] See Thompson and McEwen (81) and Thompson (80). The latter work contains the fullest discussion of environment to be found at the present.

TVA and was a contributing reason for the resignation of one of the first directors of the agency.

The strategy of cooptation is frequently utilized in organizations. There are several varieties. In political parties a vigorous but obstreperous local leader may be brought into higher positions in order to "buy him off" or, to put it less bluntly, to socialize him to the legitimacy of the policies of the dominant faction in the organization. Many industrial firms coopt representatives of their major customers, suppliers, or financial backers as the price of good relationships with these firms. These individuals are given seats on boards of directors and a say in policies which might affect the firms they represent. Once coopted, there is no assurance the group or member can be controlled completely, so in effect the controversy is moved to a different setting. But by moving it to the policy-making level the risk of wide publicity outside the organization is minimized. Voluntary and welfare associations practice cooptation when they appoint powerful people to their boards of directors who might otherwise be critical of fund-raising drives or increased taxes. The hospital will say that the members are being "educated" to the needs of the community; the outsider will add that being a board member makes it awkward for one to oppose the fund drive or higher taxes. However, one problem which can arise is that sometimes these directors have ideas of their own about running the hospital or the agency, and they may attempt to influence policy in a way that is contrary to the views of the professional managers.

One example, reported in the literature, involved a team of surgeons working in a new and exciting field. The board of directors and large donors exerted pressure upon them to release premature and misleading publicity. The researchers claimed that their standing with the foundations that supported their work was endangered and that they were swamped with applications and under pressure to work miracles on unsuitable patients before their techniques were perfected. Yet, as the administrator of the hospital put it, publicity is what the large donors buy with their donations; they like to see the facility well covered in the mass media (54).

Cooptation to secure resources or to make peace with the environment always has its price—as indeed it should. An organization that brings in a part of the social environment is making itself more responsible to that environment. We may deplore or applaud the selection—businessmen who attempt to use and cooperate with organized crime or businessmen who attempt to have representatives of "the public interest" on their boards—but no organization can ignore its environment completely. Nor can the researcher or the administrator.

Spatial and Cultural Factors

Naturally, workers, too, are drawn from the organization's environment. Studies have been made of the effect upon an organization of the background from which its personnel are drawn. One of the most striking is by Clark Kerr and Abraham Siegel (34). They examined the varying rates of strikes among industries and found consistently more strikes in certain industries, primarily mining, logging, and fishing. They argued that the social milieu of the workers was largely responsible. Workers in those industries lived in isolated areas where they had little contact with other groups. People's contacts with other groups in a differentiated community are likely to act as restraints on militant activity by providing outlets, such as channels to drain off discontent, alternative interpretations of situations, and alternative job opportunities. But in an isolated community where all workers share the same culture and interact primarily with one another, discontent is likely to become defined in a common fashion. Since there is high communication between workers, solidarity and common awareness will be promoted. Thus militancy is more possible, hence the strikes compared to such environmental factors, the role of management practices in different firms appears to be small.

The same factors can be detected in universities. Large colleges in metropolitan areas, whose faculty is dispersed in many suburbs, have less sense of academic community, tend less toward common action on university matters, and perhaps have fewer interdisciplinary contacts than those in smaller cities and towns. In the latter, it is possible and easy for faculty members to return to the campus for emergency evening meetings. Moreover, university affairs are endlessly discussed at dinner parties and other social gatherings, since most of the guests are from the university.

The environmental setting appears to affect hourly workers in other ways besides those hypothesized by Kerr and Siegel. In studying several firms in the northeastern section of the country, Turner and Lawrence (84) came upon the unanticipated finding that attitudes toward work seemed to vary systematically, depending upon the rural or urban environment of production workers. Those residing in small towns or semirural areas desired more responsibility and autonomy in their jobs than did those in large urban centers. The latter were more concerned with wages and general working conditions, such as vacations and company facilities. One presumption might be that the workers in the large urban areas found many more of their needs for autonomy and interesting activities satisfied by the urban environment, whereas those from the small town and semirural environment demanded more from their jobs. Regional differences also influence worker responses. As Robert Blauner (6) notes of textile workers in southern rural areas, they apparently demand little of their jobs in terms of interesting work or autonomy. Instead, they find many social satisfactions from working with neighbors from the community, and they show considerable community solidarity.

Of course, more extreme differences are found in contrasting workers in underdeveloped nations with workers in industrialized nations. Here the role of the environment is enormous. But even within the industrialized West large differences appear. David Granick (24) has explored such differences in culture, social structure, and governmental policies. Of more immediate interest to American firms, however, are the difficulties experienced by businessmen sent abroad by their firms to work with foreign subsidiaries or to establish branch offices or factories. They have encountered a veritable environmental nightmare where their accustomed techniques are quite inadequate, and simple communications and actions miscarry and are misinterpreted to a bizarre degree. Perhaps the most poignant victims of these international forays are the businessman's wife and family. Deprivation of the spouse's supporting environment can affect the fortunes of the husband and the firm. We might reconstruct the problem as follows:

A man is moved abroad to handle the foreign interests of his company. He takes his wife. He spends all day in the office, and many evenings too, with translators and all the props of his authority. His wife, however, has few props of her own. The language barrier restricts friendships, makes shopping hard, and managing household and servants frustrating. Unless she has a taste for adventure and languages and the flexibility to navigate in a new social world with inevitably different rules and preferences, she is likely to prefer the suburbs convenient to Dallas, Pittsburgh, Chicago, New York, or Los Angeles. Perhaps she will live in an American enclave in Paris, Rome, Brussels, or Berlin, but that is more stifling than Westchester. Hence, in addition to his own strains, the executive must deal with family strains. (Young children will further complicate matters.) Used to leaving all that sort of thing to take care of itself, he now finds himself playing a more active and unaccustomed role as a husband and head of household, and in a crisis situation. The job suffers, or the relationship, or both, and soon he is begging for a transfer back to the states. The organization, meanwhile, has invested in him a year or two which will be wasted since it takes that length of time to become effective in a different country. Consequently, corporations have adopted training programs for *wives,* singly and jointly with husbands, to cut their losses.

For a price one can hire psychologists, linguists, sociologists, and cultural experts to teach husbands and wives how to behave in foreign situations without stepping on too many toes, and above all, how to survive with the aid of only a few other nationals, the European edition of the *Herald Tribune,* and one English-language radio station.

Even if such awkward appendages as wives and children were not enough for the executive, there are the problems of incomprehensible (and always "senseless") tax laws, competitive ethics, lackadaisical suppliers, Communist unions, and the imposing state bureaucracy and state control of most European countries. (Things are worse in most under-developed countries from one point of view, but from another point of view the interloping corporation has a great deal more power.) Add to that the noncomprehension of "how things really are" by the home office, and you have a first-class business problem.

Why? Not because foreign countries are stupid or backward. It is simply that we have forgotten, or have too long taken for granted, the role of the environment in organizational affairs. Once the American executive concludes that "our way" is not the only way and adjusts to "their way," he does well enough. He may even find that there are advantages in other ways. For instance, European firms are far more centralized than are American firms. But this makes it easier to negotiate with them. The demands of the labor unions may appear irrational, but they are more often political than economic, aimed at the government more than the companies. Welfare costs are high, usually in the form of taxes, but wages are low, and destructive urban riots are few. These are only a few illustrations, and they are oversimplified, but they provide some idea of the range of environmental influences. American business is learning them fast.

Cultural Constraints on Technology

The cultural norms and values of a society set limits upon what can appropriately be done with the "raw materials" of organizations. Generally, these limitations pertain to the treatment of human beings. At one time, when it first became possible to perform lobotomies with precision, it was suggested that prisoners in penal institutions be subjected to the operation. Many lobotomies were actually performed on mental patients (and probably still are). After some outcry, the effort was abandoned in the case of prisoners and at least reduced in the case of mental patients. It has been frequently proposed in state legislatures that women who have had two illegitimate children be sterilized; the most recent attempt occurred in Maryland, spurred by fellow party members of Spiro Agnew, who was governor at the time. Presumably, this effective technique of paring the Aid to Dependent Children program has so far fallen short of full cultural acceptance.

Less well known are cultural constraints on industrial technology. Our examples are admittedly odd, and perhaps even unique, but they provide an unusual insight into the role of environmental factors in a nation that prides itself upon its unrestrained commitment to new technologies and its hard-headed dedication to efficiency.

In the late 1950s a psychopharmacologist at one of the larger pharmaceutical companies had occasion to observe about 70 women engaged in the visual inspection of drug capsules turned out by two huge, complex machines with a combined capacity of some 20 million capsules a day. The job was routine and monotonous, but it did require good visual acuity and color vision. It required no manual skill or dexterity but would have been extremely difficult to automate. So a rather large part of the payroll was expended upon this work.

The psychopharmacologist, whose job in the company was concerned with finding techniques for analyzing the effects of drugs upon animal subjects, proposed to a fellow scientist that there was an organic device available for such work which had the following favorable characteristics: a life span of 10 to 15 years, enormous learning ability, visual acuity and color vision as good as the human eye, low initial cost (about $1.50), and whose maintenance costs were "chicken feed." The device was, of course, the pigeon.[14]

---

[14] Verhave (85). I am indebted to Ernest and Julie Vargas for bringing this and the next two references to my attention.

It so happened that the company had just spent a large sum of money on a device to inspect the capsules for one defect that humans could hardly detect. Unfortunately, the device did not work. After some discussion and much joking, the scientist proceeded to design an inspection station for pigeons and to train some of them. His preliminary device turned out to be quite successful, and it was clear that the project was eminently feasible. Utilizing the "operant-conditioning" theory of psychologist B. F. Skinner—an important variant on, and improvement of, stimulus-response theory—the birds signaled for a capsule to come into view, and pressed one button with their beaks if it was defective and another if it wasn't. They were rewarded for their efforts with grain. They worked very fast, did not require rest breaks, and by arranging for two or more pigeons to inspect the same pills, the resulting accuracy was far beyond that of humans.

However, the project was killed, apparently by the chairman of the board and his brother, both elder statesmen. During their visit to the demonstration set-up they warned that salesmen from competing firms might ask doctors, "Who would trust medicine inspected by pigeons?" Says the author, Tom Verhave: "I suggested that the use of pigeons was incidental and that, for example, one could use hawks just as well; after all, what's better than a hawk's eye? This suggestion produced a wan smile." Another possible problem was that the competition might subtly suggest that the pigeons were "manually" sorting out the good and bad capsules. And, of course, there was always the Humane Society to contend with, even though it apparently could be shown that pigeons love this sort of work. The board of directors voted 11 to 1 to end the project.

In another case an engineer was complaining to a scientist about the familiar industrial problem of high-volume, high-reliability assembly machines that worked fine as long as none of the parts fed into it for assembly were defective (14). If they were, the machine would stop and mechanics would swarm all over it to find and remove the part. When people did the assembling, a tap or two with a hammer would correct the problem or the part would be cast aside without difficulty. Since the number of ways in which a part could be defective was almost infinite, it would be difficult and extremely expensive to build automatic inspection stations for all parts. One could have operators do the inspecting, but that would take all the economy out of automation.

The scientist suggested that neither people nor machines should be wasted on such a simple, visual problem of inspection; even simple animals could be trained to do that. Therefore, utilizing pigeons, he built a device for inspecting small electronic parts called diodes. Again it worked, and quite well. For example, after training, one bird averaged only one percent error while inspecting for very minute defects at a rate of over 1,000 pieces an hour. If two birds were put on the same pieces, the error would be infinitesimal. But once again the project was killed by top management. Aside from possible problems from pigeon lovers, the reaction of organized labor had to be considered. Probably more basic was the cultural attitude about use of animal labor and a feeling about the incongruity of animal labor in areas of highly sophisticated technology. Zenith may be able to convey a sense of high quality by referring to its television sets as "handcrafted," as distinct from the utilization of printed circuits and other automated devices. It would probably not induce confidence to add, "Inspected by pigeons." Yet we praise and trust the Seeing-Eye dog; nor do we object to oxen pulling carts or horses carrying people. Evidently the ancient ways of utilizing animal labor are not as incongruous as a drug firm or electronics company using animals.

There have been experiments, or at least experiments have been suggested, regarding the utilization of a small species of apes for picking fruit from trees in California. This is backbreaking work for a man, requiring so little skill as to be demeaning to humans in this age of affluence and our cultural demand for dignified, satisfying work. Apes can perform the job well and would not suffer. Apes in the orchards would be better off than those in monkey cages in the thousands of zoos across the country. But "ape-picked peaches"? And what about the people thrown out of work?

Perhaps the most ingenious and startling use of animals—pigeons again—was suggested by B. F. Skinner himself and was tested during World War II (76). This scheme was a means of using a pigeon as a homing device built into a missile dropped from a plane. It would be aimed at a target and, observing the target on a screen, the pigeon would peck at it, thus triggering guidance devices. In the final version, which worked very well in complicated laboratory simulations with a missile called the Pelican, three pigeons were used to ensure further accuracy. Finally, a committee of 12 physical scientists met to pass on the project. For a while, things went very well. Skinner felt they lost their case when the committee insisted upon removing the cover of a black box in order to actually observe a pigeon going about his work in a simulated run. Despite the intrusion of peeping, chattering humans and the extreme loss in screen illumination, the pigeon performed perfectly, as always. "But the spectacle of a living pigeon carrying out its assignment, no matter how beautifully, simply reminded the committee of how utterly fantastic our proposal was." There was considerable merriment, and the case was lost. Even if the scientists had been swayed, can you imagine the reaction of Air Force generals? Pigeons indeed!

The Environment of Other Organizations: Reciprocity and Competition

Reducing Uncertainty through Reciprocity

We are only beginning to study the most salient aspect of an organization's environment—the other organizations that influence it as competitors, suppliers, customers, unions, or regulatory agencies. For large public and private organizations the web of such relationships is vast and complicated. Generally these relationships constitute an attempt to reduce uncertainty. Oil companies frequently own substantial parts of other oil companies which, in theory at least, are in competition with them. "Conglomerates"—superorganizations like Litton Industries or Textron that own a wide variety of companies—enjoy the benefits of evening out fluctuations in demand and profitability. As noted, major suppliers and customers are often represented on the boards of corporations, possibly at the expense of the consumer or at least of the "free market." What was once called "kickbacks" or "back scratching" has now been given a far more legitimate designation—reciprocity.

Most large companies both buy from and sell to other large companies. Railroads ship steel, but they also purchase it. A large materials company needs a new building; the building contractor can either buy the necessary materials from this company or from others. Large, diversified firms have numerous opportunities for exercising reciprocity; one division has a contract for armored aluminum personnel carriers, for which a large amount of aluminum plate must be purchased, while another division makes soda ash and caustic, which are used to make alumina. The man who exploits these opportunities is called the trade-relations man; now such specialists even have a professional association. When the conglomerate, FMC Corporation, called upon Reynolds Metals to discuss their large need for aluminum plate, they also mentioned their division which makes soda ash and caustic. Reynolds said, however, that it had already made provisions for all its soda-ash requirements. FMC indicated how large their order would be, knowing that

Reynolds was troubled with excess capacity, then waited for the predictable response: Reynolds had made some change in its soda-ash requirements and now could use quite a bit of it from the FMC division (43).

Fortune cites a number of such instances, including cases in which Company A cannot reciprocate directly with Company C, but A buys from B, which in turn buys from C. So A puts pressure upon B to put pressure upon C to induce it to buy from A. In this way a chemical company was able to induce Republic Steel to buy its products by means of an intermediate who sold the chemical company large quantities of steel drums used for shipping chemicals. The intermediate bought much of the steel from Republic. All such arrangements are supposedly not influenced by price—these are cases of "all other things being equal." But, as Fortune notes, the buyer can predetermine who is going to be the low bidder by making special demands (such as specifications, delivery dates, services) that only the favored bidder can meet. Thus, the Justice Department has a hard time proving collusion in violation of antitrust laws.

The practice of reciprocity is so extensive that about 60 percent of the top 500 corporations have staff members who are explicitly assigned to trade relations. Of course, any smart sales executive or top executive can serve in this capacity. However, it is striking that the practice is sufficiently common to justify so many special positions among the giants. The importance of reciprocity probably reflects the increasing integration of our economic life or, to put it another way, it reveals the increasing centralization of economic power abetted by corporate mergers and conglomerates. Fortune notes that trade-relations men find that their jobs are easier when big conglomerates are dealing with equally big conglomerates. Of course, if the firms are of unequal size, it is the small one that reciprocates, not the large one. The practice undoubtedly does more than expand markets or increase sales under circumstances of particularly favorable profit margins. Perhaps more important, it introduces further areas of predictability and certainty for the organizations involved, which is to say it reduces unrestricted competition. But, says Fortune, competition from new products and processes—that great solvent of concentrated power according to the ideology of business—can prevent the American economy from becoming "completely dominated by conglomerates happily trading with each other in a new kind of cartel system."

Much more commonplace and typical of all types of firms is the power of the purchaser over the supplier. One of the key actors here is the purchasing agent; if he is in a large firm he can obtain all sorts of privileges and benefits from those who sell to his firm. In one case which I observed, the company was obliged to hire, during summer vacations, the incompetent and disruptive college-going son of a purchasing agent in a large firm. There was no question but that, should the man ask the firm to hire his son, they would have to do so. Gifts, football tickets, expensive entertainment at key clubs, and call girls are all part of this relationship. A great deal is at stake for the supply firm, and these costs are only a tiny fraction of the total volume of business. Large customers can also demand special services in terms of products. Because most companies do not know the true cost of "special items," they may find that they are paying a very high price to keep the customer's business by supplying him with special items or special delivery dates.

Much more dramatic than football tickets and a slot for a son during summer vacation is the matter of monopsony—dominance of the market by the buyer. The United Auto Workers called on Congress to investigate monopsony in the auto industry a few years ago, charging that Ford and General Motors forced the companies that supplied their parts to charge such low prices that the suppliers in turn were forced to pay substandard wages or to violate union contracts. The method is simple: General Motors can tell a supplier that unless his price is low enough they will make the item themselves or go to another supplier. Since, commonly, the bulk of the supplier's business is tied up in the one contract, he has little choice. Reportedly the large auto firms go so far as to send a man to the company to audit their books, tell them what the price should be, how much labor should be paid, and what kind of profit margin they will have to live with. The highly touted "efficiency" and profitability of General Motors may be, in part, due to the sacrifices of thousands of suppliers who supply close to half of the final automobile. There is little occasion for "countervailing power" here, since the suppliers are small and unorganized, while the auto companies are large and well-organized indeed.

These matters, as I have said, have not been systematically investigated by sociologists, but they are certainly within the province of sociology and we may expect to hear more about them in the future. To date, if they are considered at all they are considered primarily by economists and perhaps by political scientists. Yet they have a great deal to do with shaping the characteristics of organizations. A sharp-eyed cost accountant may go into an organization and wonder why it engages in such and such a practice; it seems so obviously inefficient. If one pursues the matter long enough one soon finds that a whole web of social relationships center about that particular activity, which no one has the temerity to disturb. The young business-school graduate may be appalled by some of the cosy relationships with competitors, customers, or suppliers, but after a few years he will learn to accept them because no one is quite sure what would happen if those relationships turned cold. With better cost-accounting information and more rational ways of doing business, a firm may be able to ferret out some of these practices and decide whether or not they are worthwhile. But many of them are not open to rational cost-benefit analysis, only to political judgments.

The Willing Suspension of Competition

When organizations have to deal with each other it is not surprising that reciprocities grow up; they benefit both firms, even though they may prove expensive to consumers and other groups. But to find cooperation among firms engaged in competition is somewhat more surprising. I do not have in mind here the cases of price-fixing and establishment of cartels; like reciprocity, these practices benefit the cooperating organizations at the expense of others. Rather, I am referring to the development of norms and sentiments that can scale down the degree of competition, with no apparent benefit, at least in the short run, to either firm. Indeed, the observer might think the costs of suspending competitive advantages are great. Yet they are suspended, because it is necessary to give moral support to the web of relationships and the norms and values that restrain struggle.

A number of strong norms exist which, from a thoroughly cynical standpoint, would be unexpected. In studying industrial corporations I repeatedly found that short-term competitive advantages were not seized by firms because "it just isn't done in this industry"; or "you might be the one in trouble next week"; or "that was a tough blow they had, and it just wouldn't be right." Take this example, from *Fortune* (91). A fire destroyed the box factory of Connelley Containers, a firm with about seven million dollars in sales at the time. But according to *Fortune*, Connelley was a prominent Roman Catholic layman and a well-liked business figure who apparently had scores of friends ready to put him back on his feet. Among them were competitors who "rallied to fill his orders, and diverted to his use $600,000 in new machinery they had on order." Within six weeks the firm was back in normal production. I observed firms lending or giving their competitors a key part of a piece of equipment to get them back into production. When they were queried about this, since competition did seem to be quite strong, the answer was generally that the other firm might do the same for them some day when something they had might burn out and a replacement was not available. Since this eventuality seemed remote, I could only conclude that there are strong norms about taking advantage of a respected competitor under certain circumstances.

Though there is a good deal of variation, in many industries the amount of plant visiting, technological talk at conventions, and reading of papers at scientific meetings suggests the kind of cooperation we would expect of social agencies rather than of competitors. Of course, papers are cleared first by the company; a man who was too indiscreet in giving away secrets in casual conversation would be warned or sacked. Nor are visitors shown everything in the plant tours. But the surprising thing is that any of this goes on at all, if one applies rational, calculating, "businesslike" criteria. Firms admit that they pick up a good deal of valuable information about competitors in this fashion.

There are probably several explanations for this behavior, including the search for prestige, but one reason must be the norms of cooperation, or at least of reciprocal sharing of information, that exist even in hotly competing industries. It is my impression that, curiously, the fewer the secrets a firm has—or perhaps, to say much the same thing, the more primitive the technology—the higher the emphasis upon secrecy. For example, basic-steel firms are more preoccupied with secrecy than those dealing with advanced special steels; glass-bottle makers are more secretive than electronics firms.

Years ago, Emile Durkheim (18) labeled these kinds of considerations the "non-contractual bases of contract," pointing out that no society could operate completely on the basis of legal and binding contracts. There must be many common norms, some give-and-take, and mutual expectations which cannot be codified. Behind these norms, however, is the threat of losing out if one does not play the game. What we have been describing is not so much selfless behavior on the part of managers and organizations, as uncertainty over what might happen if the norms were violated. This is the nature of all norms. An example is a case that I observed, in which it was not clear just what the company might risk—losing the (small) contract of a firm it supplied, losing the goodwill of others in the industry, or feeling that it was something that just shouldn't be done.

The government officials of a foreign country offered Firm A a very lucrative opportunity in their country. They wished to have more producers of a certain product and were willing to grant Firm A many concessions and to guarantee a substantial market. The firm turned the offer down; in fact, they went to considerable lengths to ensure that the offer was not informally publicized. The reason was that a division of another firm, B, was making the same product in that country. Firm A sold products to another division of Firm B. Firm A believed that if they went into competition with the foreign division of B, then Firm B might retaliate and stop buying from them. There was no guarantee that this would happen and, indeed, the purchases were not really substantial. But Firm A not only did not want to take the risk, but also felt that other companies would be critical. Not that they were unwilling to risk foreign operations; they already had a subsidiary in that country and knew there were large profits to be made. But they were so sure that it would not be a wise move that when some word of the offer leaked out, they directly informed Firm B that they would not consider entering into competition with them in that country. The young executive who had initially talked with the foreign government, and who understandably thought it was a good opportunity, would probably be more cautious the next time. It is upon such complex political as well as economic considerations that some seemingly nonrational decisions are made in apparently rational organizations.

I do not want to give the impression that all managers and all firms play the business game by informal, gentlemanly rules. Many do not; we have our "robber barons" today as we did at the end of the last century. They may have bad reputations among some businessmen, yet they prosper, attract high-quality personnel, and invite envy and admiration of at least a grudging sort from the rest of the business community. One only has to follow the court cases reported in the financial and business press to be aware of the daily charges of unprincipled, unethical, and illegal activity—cases where companies sue companies, managers sue companies, managers sue one another, or the Justice Department brings suit. Indeed, to read the *Wall Street Journal* for a week is to imagine that business is preoccupied with only three activities: mergers, quarterly financial reports, and court cases.

Charles "Tex" Thornton, the head of the fabulously successful conglomerate, Litton Industries, is a case in point. He has been the defendant in various legal actions, characterized as "unprincipled, ruthless . . . universally disliked; cannot be trusted" in a confidential report of a prestigious accounting firm and charged with falsifying requisition reports which later led to Hughes Aircraft's repayment of some $43 million to the government.[15] After Hughes fired him and his associate, Robert Ash, they immediately proceeded, with the help of a large loan from a venerable investment banking house, to purchase Litton and to move it from sales of $3 million in 1953 to $1.8 billion in 1968. Obviously, someone trusted him enough to lend him money, and it does not seem that he was universally disliked. He breakfasted frequently with Defense Secretary Robert McNamara (Litton is heavily involved in defense work), with whom he had worked at Ford when they were members of the famed "whiz kids." He has appeared on a *Time* cover and has been heralded as an example of the new breed of socially conscious businessmen. For example, Litton ran the largest Job Corps training center in the United States in 1968—but even this operation came under attack, as a result of an investigation by a government agency, for purchasing unneeded supplies from a Litton subsidiary, among other things.

Irrespective of the robber barons and the in-house suits and countersuits of the business world, our main point has been that competitive business seeks ways to deal with its environment to reduce the uncertainties of competition. Of course, it does so in many ways not discussed here, such as price-fixing, cartels, espionage, and bribery. Of particular interest to the aspiring manager, however, are the above-board strategies that are practiced openly, such as reciprocities and the suspension of competitive practices. Without an awareness of such aspects of environmental relations, the manager is likely to find that not all his competitive strategies meet with approval from top executives, nor is he likely to understand some of the practices he encounters.

Competition among Nonprofit Organizations

We might expect to find ruthless competition in the rough-and-tumble arena of private business and welcome cooperation in the quiet pastures of public welfare agencies and nonprofit organizations. Cooperation can increase the efficiency of all the organizations involved; if there is competition, it should be restricted to trying to provide better services and should not be at the expense of the client. Agencies are not threatened by bankruptcy and extinction, and collusion is, so to speak, expected. This is a planned economy, with organizations established and

[15] For a detailed description of matters mentioned in this paragraph, see Horowitz and Erlich (29).

controlled by public authorities, or closely regulated by them if they are private agencies.

Unfortunately, organizations are organizations, and the "public interest" is a concept open to almost unlimited interpretation. Walter Miller devoted an angry article to the abortive attempt to coordinate delinquency programs in Boston, Massachusetts, a few years ago (48). The petty pride, striving for prestige, competitiveness, vanity, and suspicion among organizations dedicated to the same noble goal, according to his account, was shocking. Yet the organizational analyst, familiar with the complexity of inter-organizational relationships, will put such behavior into perspective. The competition for resources is a serious and deadly game among all types of organizations, and survival is vital and not to be taken for granted.

It is not difficult for an administrator, even of a delinquency-prevention program, to conclude that cooperation with another agency, unless it is on his own terms, will threaten his autonomy and threaten the wisdom of his approach or program. We might even say that where the technology is not well developed, as in the case of delinquency prevention and juvenile rehabilitation, the basis for cooperation among organizations is most precarious. For each agency becomes wedded to its imperfect techniques, is the more defensive the more they are not demonstrably effective, and has no rational basis of proving the inferiority of competing techniques.

Even where a technology is well developed, the competition for resources and for assured survival among social or welfare agencies can be intense. Scott (67) describes such competition among agencies concerned with the problems of the blind in many urban areas, mentioning New York City in particular. The vast majority of agencies for the blind are oriented to providing service for the "attractive blind," as one might call them—the children and young adults who might be employable. The child taps the sympathy of the generous public, and the young adult promises an adequate return on investment for those who respond to more calculated arguments. Consequently, about 80 percent of the blind—the old, those with other disabilities, and those in minority groups with high unemployment rates—are more or less neglected by the agencies. With only 20 percent left, the competition to tie an "attractive blind person" to a particular agency is fierce. Since in New York City the number of agencies for the blind is large, there are barely enough clients to ensure modest-sized programs for each agency. As a consequence, once a client has "signed up" with an agency, they are reluctant to make him independent, for then the size of their program dwindles. Agencies have been accused of keeping the blind in a dependent state to justify their appeal for funds. Yet there is little effort to serve the aged blind or the totally handicapped.

All organizations compete with others for resources. The state prison is in competition with other state institutions (such as mental hospitals, reform schools, homes for the aged) when it submits its budget to the legislature. Universities compete with one another for foundation grants, government grants, faculty, and, of course, students. The student may not be aware that he is the subject of such competition, especially after he pays his fees. Nevertheless, colleges and universities are judged in large part by the quality of their product, and the quality of the "raw material" they have to work with is far more important than anything the school does in transforming it into a marketable product. Thus, the quality of a school has a high correlation with the socioeconomic status of its student body. The competition also goes on within the school, especially at the graduate-student level. A department's graduate faculty knows very well that its prestige and productivity are correlated with the quality of the students working with them, and faculty within a department compete with one another for the good students.

Hospitals compete with one another regularly for such resources as physicians, who in turn not only bring prestige, but patients—and perhaps wealthy patients—for programs, research funds, prestigious patients, good nurses. Like many business organizations, there is a critical point of activity (in this case, patient census, which is comparable to volume of production) below which hospitals lose money rapidly and above which they do quite well. Therefore, the occupancy rate is watched as closely as it is by landlords.

Most general hospitals are, of course, "nonprofit"; but this is a misleading category. One study (1), innocently sampling hospitals throughout the country in order to select some comparable ones for intensive study, came to the conclusion that very few of them were actually nonprofit, though that was their official status. The most common practice was to retain this favorable classification, in view of tax and other laws, by writing off all uncollected bills as "charity cases." However, few hospitals would take a charity case outright. Profit does not have to be paid out in the form of dividends to stockholders to be profit. It can be paid out to doctors in the form of rent-free office space; to administrators in the form of high salaries and lush perquisites; to trustees in the form of special services and rates for friends and relatives; and to all in the form of expansion and new and seldom-used equipment. (However, the pickings are not large, and one would not urge a young man ambitious for wealth to enter hospital administration.) Hospitals, like other nonprofit organizations, must deal with the same realities of organizational life as profit-making organizations—their environment is the source of the means of doing business, and there are competitors in that environment. Some way of dealing with these sources of uncertainty is the name of the game. In one case that I observed (54), several hospitals in a large city were quite annoyed when one hospital introduced, with appropriate publicity, such "gimmicks" as wine with meals and a beauty salon for maternity patients. The doctors, to whom two or three hospitals are customarily available, knew where to send their more affluent patients.

Many more examples could be given to show how nonprofit organizations compete in terms as ruthless as profit-making organizations. But enough illustrations have been provided to show that all organizations require resources, which are scarce, and must come to terms with their environment, which includes other organizations as well as the general public. Business firms appear to suspend competition more than we might expect, even as nonprofit organizations engage in more competition than we might anticipate.

Organizations and Politics

One final point about organizations and their environment must be made. Every four or five years, for the last 20 to 30 years, one business leader or another has exhorted his fellow businessmen to "engage in politics." It is their duty, they are told, and in the interest of business in general. Businessmen almost uniformly see themselves as nonpolitical, and they draw a clear and quick line between business and politics. If one uses a very narrow definition of politics—running for office, or actively supporting the campaign of one who is seeking office—this is somewhat true. But office seeking is the least important part of political activity. When the definition is expanded to include the influence of political authorities, business is very heavily involved in politics—though often unwittingly. Aside from sweeping generalities such as Schumpeter's, or highly selective and partisan political tracts by radical political writers, there have been few attempts to explore the ways in which organizations control and change their environment through political means.[16]

Most corporations have substantial power in their communities and see to it that community development proceeds along lines of which they approve. Business leaders mix with other community leaders. But even if they remain aloof, the positions which a large business would take on matters of taxation, annexation, pollution control, the location of suburbs, zoning laws, and the like are usually quite clear; powerful firms do not even need to be consulted. Businessmen fill many of the positions of leadership in voluntary groups interested in health and welfare measures. They are influential in political parties. They probably constitute the majority of the trustees of colleges and universities. As the political scene shifts from local to state and national affairs they probably have increasing power because of such factors as the increasing interdependence and complexity of the economy, the geographical and vertical mobility of the population, and the increasing power of the defense establishment which is a huge customer.

Nor can the myth of extensive and effective governmental regulation serve the myth of a nonpolitical business community. Hardly a serious study of regulatory agencies has failed to conclude that these agencies serve chiefly the interests of the large firms in the sector they are supposed to regulate.[17] Regulation is primarily aimed at increasing the predictability and security of the industry being regulated, by establishing controls that prevent certain kinds of practices. Furthermore, the small governmental staff is highly dependent upon the technical advice of specialists from the industry they are to regulate, because there are no specialists outside that industry. Finally, the ranks of regulators are infiltrated with men whose business backgrounds are in the industries being regulated and with men who will join those industries after having served a few years in the agency. Only when the agencies are quite new, or when serious scandals occur, do they seem to be vigorous in the attempt to regulate in the public interest—if, indeed, they do so then.

So, while we tend to see the environment as having an impact upon the organization, and the organization as attempting to minimize or utilize that impact, we might just as well reverse the causal sequence. Each organization is itself the environment of some other entity and as

[16] For a comprehensive survey of this topic, see Epstein (20).
[17] See, for example, the review and excellent discussion in Edelman (19, Ch. 2).

such, the organization wields power. Indeed, as we shall suggest in the next chapter, an organization is, in one sense, a unit designed to generate and exercise power, even though much of that power is exercised without thinking of it as such, or by merely taking it for granted that "this is what we should do." It is not unreasonable, for example, to argue:

> that U.S. Steel had the power to influence the patterns of racial segregation and racial practices in Birmingham, Alabama, before the city began to seethe with riots in 1963.[18] (A major employer in the city with powerful links to all political agencies can be seen as the environment of the city, instead of viewing the city as the environment of the organization);
>
> that the concrete and construction industry has the power to influence the priorities of public tax expenditures for magnificent and redundant superhighways at the expense of public transportation;
>
> that the aerospace industry has the power to influence governmental priorities for lunar exploration or anti-ballistic missile systems at the expense of such mundane problems as pollution, decaying cities, explosive racial situations, and adequate public education;
>
> that the "welfare industry" has the power to help maintain a strategy of ameliorative services to a fraction of the poor rather than attempting to undertake basic reforms in landlord practices, discriminatory retail pricing in ghetto areas, inequalities in public facilities such as garbage removal, street lighting, recreation, and pest (rat) control;
>
> that universities have long had the power to outlaw discrimination in sororities and fraternities, to refuse secret defense contracts (on the ground that the university is committed to the expansion of *public,* not secret, knowledge), to search out and support qualified students of depressed minority groups, and to teach Negro history.

The list could be multiplied for pages. It suggests the degree to which we must think of organizations as constituting the environment of other units in society, rather than merely being shaped by an environment.

---

[18] See discussion of this issue in Walton (87, pp. 156–173).

chapter
five

Organizational
Goals

The concept of organizational goals, like concepts of power, authority, or leadership, has been unusually resistant to precise, unambiguous definition. Yet a definition of goals is necessary and unavoidable in organizational analysis. Organizations are established to do something; they perform work directed toward some end. We must examine the end or goal if we are to analyze organizational behavior.

When research concerns the behavior of groups or individuals who happen to function within an organization, attention to the goals of the organization as a whole is not necessary. Much investigation that goes under the name of organizational research is of this type; it is really concerned with how groups or individuals function in certain settings. It is assumed that increasing productivity, raising morale, and reducing conflict are legitimate goals, and attention is directed toward whatever promotes these ends. But we are ultimately concerned with formal organizations rather than with group processes, so attention to the goals of the organization as a whole, or some major part of it, is necessary.

Goals, in this latter view, are problematical; it must be established that increasing productivity is, indeed, an important goal. It might appear to be obvious that all organizations seek to increase productivity, but organizations actually vary a great deal in their emphasis upon productivity (or morale, or reducing conflict). The concept of goals implies aims foregone as well as those which are sought; otherwise all that remains is a set of Boy Scout maxims. Quality may take precedence over productivity in one organization, while the reverse is true in another organization.

Among the many problems associated with the concept of organizational goals are the following: (1) It can be argued that, strictly speaking, organizations do not have goals; only individuals do. (2) Goals are hard to observe and measure. For example: should we focus upon the behavior of all members of the organization or only on the powerful ones? Should we take at face value the statement of goals of top officials, or should we ignore these and examine only what they actually do (53)? (3) How do we distinguish between a goal and a means? What one observer calls a goal, another may equally well designate as a means towards some higher or more general goal. Profit, for example, may be viewed as a goal, or as a means of rewarding stockholders or ensuring growth (the "real" goals). These and several other problems have made the goals concept one of the most ambiguous in the literature, yet it remains essential to define the ends to which organizational behavior is addressed.

For our purposes we shall use the concept of an organizational goal as if there were no question concerning its legitimacy, even though we recognize that there are legitimate objections to doing so. Our present state of conceptual development, linguistic practices, and ontology (knowing whether something exists or not) offers us no alternative.

As we examine specific organizations, we shall infer goals from a number of empirical traces. We hope that our discussion will convince the reader that the inferences are reasonable. Sometimes we will use the statements of top executives if they appear to be frank and consistent with other information. Sometimes the evidence of decisions regarding such matters as budgets, product changes, and dividend payments will be used to infer goals.

Five Types of Goals

The problem of what is a means and what is a goal will be minimized to some extent by distinguishing five types or levels of goals. But our main reason for distinguishing types of goals is to deal with the question of whose point of view is being recognized—society, the customer, the investor, the top executives, or others. For society, the justification of a steel company's existence may be to produce needed goods; for customers, the goal of a firm may be to produce certain kinds of steel and deliver them on time; for the investors, the aim may be to pay out large dividends; for top executives, the purpose may be to run a stable, secure organization where life is fairly predictable and not too stressful; for a division manager the goal may be to make the best damn steel around. From the manager's point of view, delivery, price, profits, and stability all take a back seat, just as all goals except dividends may be secondary to investors. Note that this means that organizational goals are not only multiple but may also be conflicting, and that they can be pursued all at once or in sequence.[1]

We shall distinguish five categories of goals:

(1) Societal goals. Referent: society in general. Examples: produce goods and services; maintain order; generate and maintain cultural values (52, p. 17). This category deals with large classes of organizations that fulfill societal needs. We will not discuss this group since it has little to do with functioning organizations.

(2) Output goals. Referent: the public in contact with the organization. This category deals with types of output defined in terms of consumer functions. Examples: consumer goods; business services; health care; education. Our concern will be with shifts in output categories, as when a producer of consumer goods also undertakes to train Job Corps applicants or when penal establishments seek to control the sentencing of offenders.

(3) System goals. Referent: the state or manner of functioning of the organization, independent of the goods or services it produces or its derived goals. Examples: the emphasis upon growth, stability, profits, or upon modes of functioning, such as being tightly or loosely controlled or structured. Organizations have options in these respects, and the way the system functions and what it generates irrespective of products can become goals for the members.

(4) Product goals (or, more exactly, product-characteristic goals). Referent: the characteristics of the goods or services produced. Examples: an emphasis upon quality or quantity, variety, styling, availability, uniqueness, or innovativeness of the products. Organizations vary widely and deliberately in this respect.

(5) Derived goals. Referent: the uses to which the organization puts the power it generates in pursuit of other

---

[1] This is one of the main points of a "political science" view of organizational goals, which we will rely upon, presented in Cyert and March (15).

goals. Examples: political aims; community services; employee development; investment and plant-location policies which affect the state of the economy and the future of specific communities. Organizations generate considerable power which they may use in consistent ways to influence their own members and the environment. This power is used independently of product goals or system goals.

Unfortunately, this scheme is not as neat as one might like, and some goals could be classified into one or another category. Since our major purpose is to illustrate the variety of goals organizations pursue and since some system of classification is needed to make our discussion orderly, this is not an important problem. Don't despair if you don't remember the exact difference between a system goal and a product goal; hopefully, after reading this chapter, you will be convinced that there are differences. That is the chief message.

Another complication is that it is frequently necessary to distinguish the goals pursued by investors from those pursued by management. Sometimes members of top management are the major investors, but this is not generally true in large organizations. Therefore we shall examine some cases where the system and product goals of investors and managers appear to differ.

Before discussing the categories in detail, it is useful to use the case of the National Foundation for Infantile Paralysis to provide a brief, concrete example of the categories. After polio was substantially eliminated, in part through the research sponsored by the Foundation, the organization was confronted with the question: what to do next? It considered going into mental health and a variety of other activities, but settled finally upon childhood diseases in general. This has been analyzed in the literature (74) as a case of goal succession. It was, if we consider only product goals. The shift was from one childhood disease (polio) to all childhood diseases. But from the standpoint of output goals, there was no change: the organization's goal continued to be the financing of research and limited treatment in connection with human diseases or, more generally, it was still concerned with health. In terms of system goals, there was again no change. Even though the particular task of eradicating polio was accomplished, the goal of the Foundation continued to be organizational growth, as well as to continue to operate with the same distinctive structure: a highly centralized and powerful national office and highly decentralized local leadership with open membership. Finally, in terms of derived goals, one might say that the real goal was quite otherwise; the new arrangements were merely a means of providing the Foundation's top executives with positions of power and prestige in the national health field so that they could shape the nature of the country's health activities. Shifting from polio to other diseases was merely a means to this end, as was the decision to retain the same form of organizational structure. In sum, all these goal categories are useful and relevant. Which is chosen depends upon what is to be analyzed—the health system, the shift in products, organizational growth and structure, or the power accruing to the leaders themselves.

Output Goals

Output goals, it will be recalled, refer to the general sector of the society or consumers towards which the products are directed. They include such examples as the production of consumer goods, business services, health care, and education. It is interesting to note the increasing tendency for organizations to include in their output matters which were previously handled by quite separate organizations or to add functions which had never before been performed by large, complex organizations. For example, organizations usually have some internal training program for their employees. But when an electronics company concerned with an output goal of producing an industrial product to be sold in the marketplace also undertakes to operate a Job Corps program to train the unskilled and unemployed in a ghetto area (as some companies are doing), it has added a new output goal. As we shall speculate, such an action may affect the organization in a variety of unintended ways. Most conglomerates do not change output goals when they add new products; their goal continues to be the production of goods. If such an organization begins to buy advertising companies, however, we might be inclined to say that they have added a new output goal—producing commercial services—to their original goal of production of goods.

Since a change in output goals is rare, the value of this category for organizational analysis will not be great. But it is useful for understanding the organization's relationship to the environment, national policy issues, and the nature of our "organizational society." However, even at the organizational level, attention to these goals can alert us to some massive problems of change which organizations may face. For example, prisons are becoming somewhat more involved in probation work and even crime prevention. While the "client" is perhaps the same in some cases, his location is quite different depending on whether he is in prison, on parole, or a free citizen in a crime-inducing environment. It may be difficult for prisons to think in terms other than custody and perfunctory attempts at treatment, but they are being pressured to do so. State departments or bureaus which operate prisons are beginning to argue that they should have more control over the judicial function of sentencing offenders, so that they may control their volume. Such a change is resisted on the ground that the two functions should be separate. Police departments are engaged not only in crime detection and prevention, but in social services (such as providing emergency health facilities, breaking up family quarrels, preventing self-destructive acts, and giving information and advice on a wide variety of matters). Because of these different output goals, the selection and training of a "peace" officer becomes more difficult as are supervisory practices, promotion criteria, resource allotment, and the like.

In our society there is a strong belief that organizations should not assume too many diverse functions and that if many organizations each do one of a number of different jobs, there will be healthy checks and balances. One of the bases on which liberals criticized the old company towns, where all facets of the community—religion, recreation, housing, consumer goods—were controlled by the corporation, was that industry should stick to its own output sector and leave these others in the hands of independent groups of citizens. Businessmen and conservatives attacked the Tennessee Valley Authority not only because it was competing with private business, though there the question of output goals entered since the businessmen believed the government's output goal should not include commodities like electric power and fertilizer. The attack also centered about the fact that due to the massive effects of building dams and producing cheap power and fertilizer, the TVA drew into its orbit of control large segments of planning that had always been the province of the private sector. These included such matters as the establishment of recreation areas (telling private firms in the recreation business where they could and could not set up business), the relocation of towns and people, the design of newly built towns, the uses of timber and watershed areas, the training and subsidization of independent farmers, and the farming techniques that would be employed. As in socialism, a variety of output goals were being fused into one large agency. (Due to the survival goals of TVA, most of its power in these areas was transferred to local economic and political interests, so the consequences were not as dire as businessmen had feared (68).)

This issue of the public or private control of certain kinds of output is still quite alive, though now the controversy does not center about company towns or "socialism" and federal planning. Ironically, the roles have shifted. Now the dispute concerns the intrusion of business into the public areas of education and community facilities. Liberals have criticized business for taking on the tasks of socializing and training the hard-core unemployed; for investing in, establishing, and controlling the planned communities, or "new towns"; for exercising, through business-dominated boards of trustees, too much control over the universities; for creating, in former President Eisenhower's words, a military-industrial complex, and even, in the words of Michael Harrington, a social-industrial complex (26). The issue is one of limiting organizations to certain broad output goals in the interest of a pluralistic society. Conservatives, with their cry of "creeping socialism," rail as much as liberals over this issue.

It is obvious that taking on a new function will have a considerable effect upon an organization, but we cannot go much beyond that generalization. The Ford Motor Company found it quite difficult to include even the production of appliances in its output goals, let alone training hard-core dropouts or remaking the dreary city of Detroit. Ford bought Philco as a diversification measure and fully expected to rehabilitate the sickly company through the infusion of talent and capital, which Ford had in abundance (73). Within a short time, all but three of the top 25 men at Philco had left, voluntarily or otherwise, and Ford brought in 18 young managers in the first six months, including seven at the vice-presidential level. Within four years there were about 50 Ford men working in the Philco division. But the patient did not respond to all this new blood. Henry Ford II contended that "a good manager can run anything." But, according to *Fortune,* the man now running Philco says: "This is not true, and Ford has paid a fat price to learn it." If the shift from autos to appliances is so difficult, how about the shift to social programs?

Present experience with such goals is still too limited to draw final conclusions, but it seems likely that there could be internal reverberations if the new output goals were to command very much in the way of organizational resources and talents. Routes to the top can change, and those who take the novel assignments and do them well might well achieve rapid promotion in the company. But managers who are effective in traditional roles may easily falter in novel jobs, and few may wish to take the risk. Attitudes towards "bungling, inefficient government" may change as companies experience the recalcitrance of clients or the complexities of total community planning. Those outside the corporation who decry the lack of social responsibility of business may be alarmed when they see what the product of such ventures looks like. What a business concern may conceive of as socially desirable, the liberal critic may feel is quite undesirable.

We have explored this subject at such length because it promises to be a controversial one for the next few decades. As the economy becomes more complex and interrelated, as there are more and more joint ventures of government and business, and as business expands its activities to include matters traditionally defined as belonging to the public sector, there will be shifts in output goals. One can see this shift in output taking place in the universities today. Originally concerned with training ministers, universities later assumed public-sector responsibilities, such as training teachers, doctors, and government officials. There followed an increasing number of programs for engineers and businessmen. More and more, the engineering, agricultural, and business schools began to define the output goal. Now, when the "intellectual" has become a distinct class or status group (35), the demand is that universities be concerned primarily with knowledge rather than with training. In this view their clients are not the churches, public schools, and corporations, but society as a whole. Social commentary and criticism are held to be the vital tasks, rather than training. Such a shift in goals will be hard won, if it is to occur, and perhaps it can only be accomplished by means of specialized institutions that will train intellectuals to continually subject society to critical analysis. At the same time, most universities and colleges will continue to train the specialists needed to man a high-energy technology and a complex society. But there is no doubt that in the meantime this controversy over the proper goals of universities contributes to an unprecedented turnover of university presidents, who are caught between the demands of business-oriented trustees and legislators, on the one hand, and faculty and student intellectuals, on the other.

Investors and Managers

Every organization, public or private, economic or nonprofit, has investors. Someone has to provide capital to get the organization going, and someone has to "own" or be legally liable for it. Sometimes the power of investors is highly concentrated—a single individual or a family may own a firm; a legislative committee may oversee a government agency. At other times ownership is widely dispersed—no one owns even as much as two or three percent of the stock, or the affairs of the agency are supervised by the legislature as a whole. If stock is widely dispersed in an economic organization, the board of directors acts as representatives of the investors, through the device of proxy voting. They may or may not represent the interests of the many investors; indeed, they may be operating managers of the firm as well as directors. As operating managers, their interests may diverge from those of investors—they may seek stable, risk-free operations whereas investors might prefer risk taking, with the chance of an increase in the market value of their stock. Whether investors have influence over organizations and whether they even seek influence, then, depends upon a number of complex factors. Even in a private agency run by, say, a board elected by a religious group which sponsors the organization and helps meet its deficits, the board may be either active or passive. The real control, in fact, may lie with the United Crusade or Community Chest, who parcel out to the agency some of the funds collected from the community in the name of hundreds of other agencies along with this one.

In the case of social welfare organizations, the "investors" are legislators or other public agencies or "authorities," who grant the organization a charter (permission to exist and do business, within certain constraints), provide funds for capital investment and operating costs, review annual reports of activities and expenditures, and choose the chief executive officer when necessary. As far as setting positive goals is concerned, such investors may be very passive. In many cases it is enough that the organization exists, as evidence that "something is being done" about incarcerating criminals, helping delinquents, controlling mentally ill people, or dealing with the needs of deprived groups. Beyond this, the investors hope only that the enterprise will not cost too much and that they will not be forced to become involved because of scandals. Not all investors act this way, of course, and there are many examples of intervention in the affairs of agencies by legislators or commissions who are too strict or too lenient, too conservative or (more likely) too radical. Such intervention may occur even in the absence of riots, escapes, publicized beatings, welfare chiseling, promotion of radical doctrines, or other scandals.

Earlier we discussed a private hospital that had found that large donors expected wide publicity concerning the results of their donations. These benefactors viewed this particular product as a source of prestige. At the same time, the researchers who built and used the equipment wished to minimize publicity in order to stave off unsuitable patients and to protect their reputations with other doctors and with the federal agency which had also helped finance the project. Their product goal was quality and integrity. This conflict over the characteristics of the product had manifold consequences for the hospital. The case could also be analyzed as a conflict between two sets of investors—the private donors and the government agency—both of which had in mind their own separate and quite different "returns" or goals for the hospital.

When one thinks of investors as exercising positive direction on the development of an organization, the most commonplace example that comes to mind is the family-owned business. The investor and the manager are often one and the same. The second most obvious example is the firm where members of management own or control enough stock (10 percent will generally do if no one else owns more) to control the company. While we tend to regard such organizations as typically small we shall see that quite a few of them make the *Fortune* list of the 500 largest industrials. Small or large, there is still some value in conceptually separating the interests of managers as investors from the interests of the same individuals as managers. There is the question of the "patrimony" in the family-owned business—the existence of resources that belong to the family and can be employed in the interests of the family. This goal may conflict with the interests of the organization. Most notably, the organization can provide secure positions with status, income, and a socially legitimate role for children and other relatives, such as brothers, nephews, and sons-in-law who are employed by the firm. The importance of doing this should not be disregarded; one of the advantages of owning a business is that you can provide respectable positions for relatives and children. Furthermore, ownership is kept intact and not subject to a raid (an increasingly worrisome possibility for businesses during a time when the merger rate is high). Relatives can be trusted more than strangers or acquaintances, and trust is vital in the world of corporate secrets and internal factions. Security is important not only to protect technology, products, special markets, and salary information which might invite manpower raids, but also to protect the firm in its legitimate and illegitimate varieties of tax evasion. "Professional management" has somewhat reduced the need for loyalty in organizations, but no more than kings and dictators can corporation executives sleep completely soundly. When relatives are involved, there is an increment of trust beyond what is probable with acquaintances and strangers.

However, this kind of loyalty, plus the ability to keep an estate intact are bought at a price. Family-dominated firms appear to be continually weighing the advantages of this basis of control against the resulting loss of efficiency, talent, objectivity, and, sometimes, flexibility. We noted earlier that there is no guarantee that the son of a successful entrepreneur will inherit his father's talents. Thus, the goals of investors can conflict with the goals of others in the organizations. The existence of family dynasties in politics and government reminds us that the phenomenon is not limited to business concerns.

Beyond such speculations it is difficult to determine the consequences of family-oriented goals in organizations. For example, according to *Fortune* (72), a very conservative estimate indicates that at least 150 of the 500 largest industrials are controlled either by one man or a family. Yet, on the basis of *Fortune's* data, these 150 corporations do not seem to be distinguishable from the other 350 in terms of risk taking, profitability, growth, and other such factors. We cannot say that they are more stable, more conservative, or less innovative than the others. Some have had low-quality sons or relatives as presidents, but some have drawn outstanding executives from the controlling family. Indeed, businessmen commonly note that as long as a few, perhaps only two, key slots are filled with competent people, all manner of incompetence can be endured in other key slots. Chief executives are frequently not so important, and the bewildering nomenclature of top management allows the real leader to hide under such titles as Chairman of the Board, Chief Executive Officer, President, Executive Vice-President, Group President, or Senior Vice-President. Any one of these dignitaries can be the real power behind whatever title is given to the throne.

It is worth noting, by the way, that the remarkable finding that at least 30 percent of the top 500 industrials are controlled by one man or a family comes at a time when we take for granted the separation of ownership from control for all but a few oddities like Ford or DuPont. The dilution of stockholder control, the rise of "professional management," and the emergence of the conglomerate corporation hardly would portend so high a percentage of family-run businesses. (Professional management does not literally mean that management has necessarily become a profession or that these companies are run by college-educated managers who take a professional viewpoint. It only means that management is their vocation, and they do not own a significant fraction of the stock of a company.) No trend data are cited by *Fortune*, but it is clear that just as some firms pass out of the control of a family, others come under family control. Therefore, we cannot be sure that the figure will decline further.

There are no conclusive findings on how the goals of investor-controlled firms might differ from the goals of those controlled by professional managers. But a long list of commentators, from Adolph Berle and Gardiner Means (4) and Robert A. Gordon (22) in the early 1940s to John Kenneth Galbraith (21) in 1968, would argue that investor-controlled firms seek to maximize such system goals as profits whereas those dominated by professional managers seek to maximize growth and security. Recent research has left unclear whether owner-controlled firms are more or less profitable than manager-controlled firms, but such information would not tell us about goals, only performance. It seems clear that owner-controlled firms, whatever their emphasis upon profit maximization, have managed to grow well enough, and many are indistinguishable from manager-controlled firms insofar as goals can be determined.

System Goals

System goals pertain to desired conditions of the organization as an organization, rather than to the goods or services it produces. A high rate of profit for the organization would be a system goal, as would a high rate of growth. An emphasis upon stability for the organization is a system goal—it says something about the organization as a whole—and this emphasis varies by organizations. Some other typical system goals are an emphasis upon a particular kind of structure or process—e.g., some organizations are committed to centralized, bureaucratic, tight-ship operations for their own sake, while others are not. Rapid product change or innovation, or being judged an industry leader, are possible system goals. Managers have choices in these matters and can say: "This is the best way for this organization to function." To some extent, some system goals are simply constraints—survival is not a preoccupation of most successful organizations, but it is a necessity for any organization if it is to be an organization. But for some organization, what might have been a constraint can become a goal in itself, and organizational behavior is thereby affected. Organizations, of course, can also choose not to survive, but we are more likely to know about those which survive than about those which do not.

For economic organizations the major areas in which goals are established, relating to the system or organization as a whole, concern stability, fiscal policies, size and growth, method of internal operation, and relationship to the environment. The decisions taken in these areas may be clear-cut determinations by one man or an executive team, or they may result from incremental policies built up over a long period of time, where "no one really decided it; it just came to be the way things are done here." But they are important decisions; they are difficult to change; change would generally involve some internal pain and substantial adjustment, and they often provide a shorthand clue to the character of the organization.

Stability and Risk

Stability may subsume several of the other goals, but is worth emphasizing in its own right. Some organizations place a premium upon stable operations, few risks, and gradual and incremental change. Generally, their technology and market situation makes this feasible, or even dictates it. If an organization has enormous "sunk costs"—fixed investments which are relatively immovable—or resources which can only be exploited over a long period of time, as in mining, there will be a corresponding emphasis upon stability in all phases of the operation and in fiscal and even community areas. The railroads were in such a position until trucks and airlines began cutting in on their monopoly; many of them still behave as if there were no competition. Those rails which have emphasized and risked change and have sought innovations not only in technology but in organizational structure and in relationships with the environment of communities, competitors, customers, and regulatory agencies, have done so with high consciousness of their maverick status in the industry.[2] Incidentally, even though the railroads are saddled with inefficient and inflexible rate structures, overregulated, and generally out of tune with current transportation needs, they are not necessarily unprofitable. They have enormous reserves in land and other capital investments which make them truly sleeping giants. While their return on investment is small, their net profit is quite respectable. The net income as a percent of operating revenues of the seven largest in 1966 was 11.4 percent, quite good for an ailing and wailing industry.

On the other hand, some industries cannot expect to survive without the system goals of change, innovation, and risk. In this connection, one frequently hears, "If we have been doing it the same way for five (or two) years, we must be doing it wrong by now." An organization with this attitude places a premium on change or even makes a virtue of change, rewarding it for its own sake. Lines of communication

[2] See the fascinating account of Southern Railways in Meyers (47).

must be flexible and open and in steady use; investment risks are considered to be part of the overhead. One expects them and hopes that there will not be too many.

An organization which lives with and accepts risks adopts a different criterion of performance from one which does not. In such organizations the statement may be heard that if a man has not made a few bad and costly decisions, he is probably not making enough decisions, or taking enough risks. At times this heretical criterion is employed in hospitals among doctors. They say there should be a certain (small) percentage of cases where the examination of tissue removed during surgery reveals that the organs were not, in fact, diseased and there was no need of surgery. The argument is that unless this happens, some patients will suffer or die because the doctor was uncertain and reluctant to order surgery, when in fact it was necessary. Similar reasoning is employed by sophisticated social agencies. If there are no instances of "welfare chiselers," then too much money is being spent on determining eligibility and on policing; such a situation is uneconomical. It may also mean that the organization is only handling very sure "risks" and thus not offering service to others who need it; allowing for a small percentage of clients who may be misusing aid is considered a small price to pay for complete coverage.

This willingness to take and live with risks may seem ridiculous to those who favor a highly stable and conservative system. Such people need several very good reasons for taking a new step, but only one for not taking it. This position is realistic if the organization is very secure or if risky actions can be extremely dangerous. The position is also popular, of course, with those who stand outside the organization and demand of it a perfect decision record. It is hard to justify errors that may serve the organization in some vague "long run."

Fiscal Policies

Fiscal policies can also achieve the status of system goals. Organizations vary in their viewpoint on financial matters. Some organizations believe it is folly not to have a substantial debt. Not only does borrowed money provide more flexibility and resources, but it is a sign of a healthy and growing organization—a judgment shared by the lending agencies. For others, debt is avoided as if the depression were around the corner. This policy was said to have nearly ruined Montgomery Ward during the reign of Sewell Avery. For example, although DuPont is an innovative and risk-taking organization in many respects, it maintains a very conservative fiscal policy. It is in a position to generate a substantial amount of capital internally, but outsiders have argued that it could do more if it increased capital expenditures, particularly since it could borrow the funds at very low rates. When pressed on this issue by several economists a few years ago, I heard the treasurer of DuPont finally fall back on the seemingly nonresponsive answer that the lack of significant debt allowed the treasurer to sleep better at night. This reply was not entirely irrelevant for the company, since it reflected the in-grained attitude of a long succession of executives from the DuPont family, a point of view whose origin was in severe fiscal problems in the dim past. As a consequence, DuPont has required a higher estimated rate of return on new investments (in products, new plants, new methods) than its competitors, and its competitors have grown faster than DuPont. In the mid-1960s there were signs that this system goal might be changed, for the company had lost its commanding leadership position.

To illustrate fiscal goals in more detail, we will examine two cases drawn from the corporate stories in *Fortune* magazine. Several will be used in this chapter since they are graphic and insightful characterizations. But we should note that we are relying upon journalistic accounts. The first illustrates the goal of cost reduction, the second, maximizing returns to investors.

EASTERN AIRLINES

Even though he owned only three percent of the stock (no one owned more), it was quite clear that Eddie Rickenbacker, the World War I ace, controlled Eastern Airlines from 1935 to 1959 and ran it as if he owned it all. No one was disposed to quarrel with his leadership, for the company was the most consistent money-maker in the volatile airline business. For 25 years it had a record of uninterrupted profits; this included very large gains at a time when the other airlines were losing money. According to *Fortune*, Rickenbacker ran a one-man show, and the main act was economy: "Despite his dashing war record and flam-boyant exterior, he had the cautious soul of a greengrocer when it came to spending money." His frugality became an industry legend. He actually lectured his employees on the importance of saving not just pennies, but mills (a mill is one-tenth of a cent). His main goal for the company appeared to be cost reduction, and it worked for a good many years.

Organizations are likely to be particularly concerned with cost reduction when they are in a monopoly situation. Further expansion of the monopoly is risky, but a dynamic leader can always stress cost reduction. Since the market is more or less guaranteed, this becomes a significant lever. Many public agencies operate in this environment—their market or domain is established by some parent body, such as the legislature, and they are expected to carry out the mandate at the lowest possible expense to the public. Eastern was in such a situation, with a near monopoly on its most profitable routes, particularly the lush New York–Miami run. Its only competitor there was small and could not field as many flights as Eastern. For Eastern, its route structure meant that it was easy to make money as long as costs were kept under control, and this is what Rickenbacker did.

However, cutting costs meant reducing services. The airline was slow in introducing faster and more comfortable aircraft, which started to come along every three or four years. Tight scheduling, to ensure maximum use of aircraft, and careful control of maintenance saved money, but this meant that scheduling and maintenance were at the convenience of the company, not the customers, and less desirable departure and arrival times were utilized. Service aboard the plane was spartan; given the cost of a ticket, the saving on a midmorning snack was really pinching pennies. Coffee and cookies were served instead of breakfast. Seating was five abreast in contrast to four on other lines. While other airlines were hiring pretty stewardesses, Eastern retained male stewards on the grounds that they could perform a wider range of duties and would not give up their jobs to get married. Errors in reservations were frequent, as was overbooking. Airlines count on some no-shows, and therefore on some runs they sell more seats than they have. But Eastern did it more frequently and blatantly. In one celebrated instance *nine* more passengers than could be accommodated showed up with confirmed reservations. Seven of them accepted their fate stoically, but two decided they had had enough of this treatment from Eastern. They stood under the plane's propellors for more than an hour, preventing take-off. (You can understand how the airport security guards might be reluctant to drag away forcibly two businessmen in front of a gathering crowd.) The newspapers covered the story, and soon an informal organization called WHEALS—We Hate Eastern Air Lines—came into existence and appealed to the Civil Aeronautics Board.

Meanwhile, the competition, investing in newer planes, nonstop service conveniently scheduled, pretty girls, and good food started to cut into Eastern's near-monopoly. The final straw was the decision of the Civil Aeronautics Board to strengthen smaller lines and competition by giving them a chance at the more profitable and busy routes. This step affected all large airlines, but Eastern was already performing poorly. With old equipment, poor service, and inconvenient schedules at Eastern, the interlopers did well and Eastern started to go under. The line lost increasing amounts of money from 1960 to 1963, and its share of trunk-line traffic was cut by one-third. Rickenbacker had retired in 1959, just before the deluge. In 1964, he commented, with his usual crispness: "It took 25 years to build Eastern and only three and a half years to tear it apart."

Rickenbacker held the largest single block of stock in the corporation, and his investment had grown enormously over the years. He had been able to run the organization as if he owned it all and to pursue the system and product goals that he desired (for example, low-cost operation as a system goal, and minimal service as a product goal). An interim executive did what he could from 1959 to 1963, but Rickenbacker was still active as chairman of the board. The new executive introduced innovations, such as the shuttle service out of New York, and he managed to secure massive refinancing. But it was only after Floyd Hall took over in 1963, and Rickenbacker had left the board, that company policies and system and product goals were changed. Hall did not own a substantial interest in the company and thus did not have much interest in high dividends and short-term profits. He bought new planes and introduced nonstop routes, substantially increasing debt; sold off unprofitable feeder lines; stressed customer service (reducing short-run efficiency), and undertook the then unsentimental and unusual step of changing the advertising agency in order to create a new image. The "new look" at Eastern paid off, and remarkably quickly. The worst year had been 1963; *Fortune,* writing in 1964, estimated that it might lose 15 million dollars in 1964, while the new president dared hope for only a five million dollar loss. It turned out to be 5.8 million dollars. The profit in the next year, 1965, was a handsome 29.7 million dollars. The company has not done as well since. Its ten-year growth rate in earnings is still far below the big four, ranking about eleventh among the airlines, according to figures for 1967. Still, it managed to make 24 million dollars in 1967.

One way to look at this example is to say that the airline was mismanaged by Rickenbacker and allowed to get out of step with the times. From this viewpoint, the company's goal was and continued to be high profits. But this tells us little; it says Eastern's goals were just like the goals of other airlines, and the difference was that they used different means. Eastern's methods no longer worked in the 1960s, so it changed them. But referring to means and "poor management" only begs the question. Nor does the line's near-monopoly status explain too much. As Joseph Schumpeter once pointed out, the only successful monopoly is one that does not behave as if it is a monopoly. Furthermore, the other large airlines had their own protected routes.

A more telling explanation would be that mismanagement was not the problem and that, rather, the system goal pursued by Rickenbacker deserved analysis. Given the goal of maximizing profits through cost reduction, his preoccupation with frugality served the company extremely well for 25 years. Had the environment not changed and had his successors continued his policy, there would have been no question that the company had been extremely well-managed. The other airlines, we presume, had no such goal. For them, profit itself, from a short year-to-year perspective, appeared to have been more of a constraint on their activities, and not a very strong one, at that. *They* pursued goals of growth and innovation. We know very little about the other companies, but it does not appear that they were all mismanaged while Eastern made money, or that they were all well-managed when Eastern lost money. The other companies simply had different goals, and when their goals of growth and product innovation began to pay off, Eastern had to change its goals, too (65).

TEXAS GULF SULPHUR

In the case of Texas Gulf Sulphur we have a similar instance of change in system goals and the way they affect an organization. Here the goal was to maximize the immediate return to investors. Texas Gulf was organized early in this century, when the basic patents on a revolutionary and cheap method of extracting sulphur ran out (this was the Frasch process, whereby superheated water is pumped into a sulphur "dome," thus melting the sulphur). With money from J. P. Morgan and Bernard Baruch, and the latter's organizing skill, the company was soon one of the two largest sulphur firms in the world. The selling price of the two firms was soon identical, and the money rolled in for more than three decades. At its peak, Texas Gulf had remarkable net profits of 35 percent on sales of almost 100 million dollars (most companies are in the five to 10 percent range). There was no need to diversify or to worry; sulphuric acid was vital for the basic industries of industrialized countries. One man ran the company from 1919 to 1951, and continued as chairman of the board for another six years, until he was 89 years old. His successor continued his policies, the most important of which was to pay out an average of 80 *percent* of earnings in dividends. The rest was retained in cash, and in some years the working capital (cash) was higher than the volume of sales. The company even turned down the rights to a rich Mexican field because it did not want to exceed its small sulphur exploration budget. This was the beginning of the end of *that* goal—high dividends and extreme liquidity.

Then an upstart company, formed by some adventurers and, after Texas Gulf turned them down, financed by some wealthy Texas oilmen as a lark and a means of tax savings, started production in Mexico and broke the monopoly of the two dominant companies. These two cut prices, but so did the new company. The result was simply lower oligopoly prices for all. During World War II and again in the Korean War, a world-wide sulphur shortage developed (which could have been exploited by the two dominant producers, but wasn't), and so France and Canada went into the business and began producing. Earnings per share for Texas Gulf went from $3.25 in 1955 to $1.27 in 1960. Enter a new chief executive officer (Claude Stephens) and a change in goals.

Says *Fortune:* "Though it would perhaps be an exaggeration to say that Stephens had been leading a Young Turk movement in Texas Gulf [while he served as president for three years before gaining full control], he was obviously itching to institute change." In a "complete turnabout in policy" he slashed the dividend rate from a dollar a share to 55 cents and then to 40 cents. He took the 300 million dollars in cash in the treasury (an incredibly high figure for a company with sales of 70.4 million dollars at the time), raised another 30 million, and spent it on developing new properties and phosphates. The company, which had been accustomed to spending around five million dollars a year in capital expenditures, planned, in 1964, to spend 100 million dollars at the least in the next three years.

What had taken place? One could say that before Stephens the company was poorly managed and the only change was, not in goals, but in tactics. If goals are to be specified in such general terms as survival and profit, the statement is true, but unenlightening. Since almost all firms have goals of survival and profit, we learn little about particular organizations from this observation. It is more instructive to say that in response to a drastic change in the environment (supply, demand, and competition), there was a drastic change in goals: from high investor return and liquidity to growth and diversification. (Under Stephens, Texas Gulf is diversifying in related areas to reduce its dependency upon the ups and downs of the sulphur market and to capitalize upon the related minerals and products that go with sulphur mining and refining.) The dividend rate is now a constraint upon the use of profits for expansion. A "fair return" to investors must be provided to keep them quiescent, but this is no longer the dominant goal. Risk taking and deficit financing are now acceptable policies in view of the goals of growth and diversification. Presumably, any highly placed manager in Texas Gulf had better take this shift to heart, or he will have trouble adjusting (71).

Growth

Growth is another possible system goal. Again DuPont provides an example. The company executives repeatedly stress, in their official statements to security analysts and other influential groups, that growth is not a goal of DuPont; instead, their goals are profitability and a high return on invested capital. In doing so they implicitly and sometimes explicitly contrast themselves with those firms that are regarded as the very models of progressive management. Growth has become such a preoccupation of American business and is held by so many commentators to be the true goal of professional managers, that it is well to remind ourselves of firms like DuPont. Growth comes at a cost, and some firms are not willing to pay the price.

In my experience, many family-controlled manufacturing firms of modest size (around 30 to 50 million dollars in sales volume) are glad to grow *if* growth doesn't make life too difficult, cause them to be targets for mergers, dilute their control of the stock if the firm is public, force them to go public if it is not, or threaten their ability to ensure high corporate positions for sons and relatives. In view of all these risks, growth is not very highly valued. Yet these firms can be quite profitable, well managed, and even exciting places in which to work. (One cannot climb too high in them, however, for they will probably remain small, and a vice-presidency in a modest-sized firm is not as "high" in status as a department head in a large firm.)

Of course, growth is desirable for many other reasons. It is a validation of success and thus a sign of prestige. Perhaps incorrectly, it suggests security for all concerned. It certainly provides status escalators for managers, since it opens up promotions. It makes the top-management positions higher because, as the pond grows larger, so does the size of the frog. It provides more options for talent, as well as more places to hide whenever more sophisticated younger people come along. As the economy grows, there is room for all organizations to grow. But should the economy falter in the future, we may find that other criteria are held up by social scientists as the goal of the professionally managed firm. Growth may appear at the present time to be an inevitable goal of professionally managed firms in the view of social scientists, merely because it was achieved with relative ease in the 1960s.

Method of Operation

In some organizations the method of operation achieves the status of a goal; it becomes something to be protected at all costs and is seen as an end in itself. The statement, "We believe in running a tight ship here," is reinforced by personnel policies, structural arrangements, and by other means, so that when the organization needs to loosen up to adjust to change, it finds it can't alter the commitment to this system goal. (Other organizations, of course, have no such commitments and thus no goals in this area.) General Motors was apparently so profoundly affected by the revolutionary changes in structure carried out by Alfred Sloan in the 1920s that its decentralization of operations, with centralized fiscal and policy controls, has become an article of faith. Since General Motors does all right in its gargantuan way, and since these policies may indeed still have a great deal to do with its performance, there is no need to change.

But across the street, Ford Motor Company has pursued a quite different strategy for much of its stormy life. At one point it hired away a top G.M. executive with the avowed intention of modeling itself upon the G.M. organization. Somehow, while the whole structure was adapted in many aspects, it did not work, or at least it did not "take." Ford is an "open system" corporation, so to speak, where a man can move up rapidly if he is aggressive and makes a couple of highly visible, good decisions, and where he can go down or out just as rapidly as a result of one bad move. At G.M. such a posture would be heresy. People rise slowly; presumably, top-notch talent is stacked three or four deep behind every position of at least moderate importance—where they wait. (Of course, at G.M., this is well-paid waiting. With its commanding position and high profits it can afford this practice.) People are not fired; they are just moved aside. Some saw the costs of such a philosophy appearing in performance reports in the late 1960s. Ford had the jump on G.M. with Thunderbirds, Falcons, and Mustangs; G.M. found it must respond to Ford, rather than the other way around. Ford managers spoke of a policy of flexibility and of hit-and-run guerrilla warfare in the product line, while they tried to out-distance G.M. in the "Buck Rogers stuff" of econometric models of the firm and elaborate dealer-inventory simulation studies (11). It is clear that quite different managerial styles are operating here, and it would appear that General Motors' style has been entombed as a system goal.

Environmental Stance

Another area where there may be a system goal in operation (or, as others might call it, a basic strategy) is the matter of relationship with the environment. Is the environment to be seen as a sink into which the products one desires to make are dumped, or is it to be viewed as a source of ideas or demands for products that one might be able to make (10)? Quite different postures are involved here. For some organizations, the first is perfectly sound, while for others it would be disastrous. The problem comes when the first is no longer appropriate, and the firm finds it cannot shift to the second. This was the case with the Endicott Shoe Company, which made excellent shoes that no one wanted and which were sold through outlets that were no longer strategic (39). Endicott was constructed around the perception of the environment as a place where it could dump its products. The structure and training of the sales force, the manufacturing facilities, the attitude toward long-term debt, all were based upon the value of this way of viewing the environment. Thus, what had once been a matter of strategy or tactics had become, of necessity, an end in itself, just as growth or short-run profitability can be a goal.

We can see something of this in the case of Consolidated Edison of New York, the nation's largest gas and electricity utility. There, the strategy of controlling the environment by means of neutralizing its political forces has become a goal of the organization, in contrast to another utility, where expansion of customer services is the goal. Con Ed, as it is called, grew out of a potpourri of gas, steam, and electric utilities in the 1930s. The utility immediately ran into trouble with Mayor Fiorello La Guardia, an advocate of public power, who constantly threatened to have the city go into competition with Con Ed in order to force rate reductions (51). In fact, three publicly owned systems were supplying power to the subway system, a very large user. Rather than meet the challenge through rate reductions and increased service, Con Ed plunged into city politics, hiring a man who could develop close relationships with city hall. This man, who had risen to the position of chief executive officer long before the time of the *Fortune* story, was Charles Eble. As he puts it, somewhat disingenuously: "Over the years I struck up friendships with many politicians. It was not something that I set out to do objectively at the beginning. But, as time passed, I found that many of my friends had moved into positions of authority in government. I could talk to them. It was as simple as that."

But politics is not as simple as that, and while Eble was frequently visiting politicians in Washington and Albany, where he was on good terms with leaders of both parties, two vice-presidents also had as their major responsibilities the task of dealing with city and state legislators. One of these vice-presidents had a strong link with the powerful Central Labor Council. (Because of its continual maintenance and construction program, Con Ed provides between 15 and 20 percent of the jobs for building-trades workers in New York.) The other vice-president is said to have had "a sixth sense about where the centers of power lie," and he handled special political assignments. Another key figure was a consultant who was a long-time associate of Carmine DeSapio, a former Tammany Hall leader who has sometimes been linked to the underworld. Consequently, Con Ed is heavily involved in the clubhouse politics of both parties.

Perhaps as a consequence of this strategy of dealing with the environment, Con Ed has the worst earnings record, service record, and general public relations of the utility industry. As *Fortune* puts it, its "deficiencies are legion" (in all respects except its political power). Power interruptions are frequent, rates are extremely high, equipment is medieval, and it has been rebuked by Federal Power Commission (which takes some doing). The longevity of its officers is remarkable; in 1966 the top 21 officers had been with the company an average of more than 33 years apiece. The three top officers were 65, 64, and 63 years of age. By buying security through political relationships, Con Ed has apparently not had to worry about its deficiencies.

Utilities are in a monopoly situation, and this explains a great deal, but they do differ in their relationships with their environment and other system goals. In contrast to Con Ed, consider American Electric Power Company, covering what would apparently be a quite unprofitable area. Its territory includes much of depressed Appalachia and has only four cities of over 100,000 population: Fort Wayne, South Bend, Canton, and Roanoke (33). Yet the company generates and has sold more electric energy than any other company in the world (Con Ed is the largest company providing both gas and electric power). American Electric Power has been steadily lowering its rates, raising the quality of its service, and aggressively promoting its product. At the time of the *Fortune* article, in 1966, it had raised its dividends every year for 11 years and in the last year threw in a stock dividend to boot. Meanwhile, its rates run from 25 to 38 percent below the nation's average. As a consequence it has attracted power-hungry industry, including aluminum, and has promoted all-electric homes. Its forte has been research and development; it was headed by an electrical engineer, Philip Sporn, from 1947 to 1961, whom *Fortune* touts as the "mass-producing, cost-cutting Henry Ford of electric power." It has continually introduced innovations in such areas as heat pumps and high-voltage transmission. We may surmise that Sporn did not rely upon his knowledge of state legislators and city machines to ensure the growth and profitability of the company. He "retired" at age 65 but was still active in the system development committee of A.E.P. four years later. He was succeeded by an outsider, Donald Cook, who had come to the company eight years before from his position as chairman of the Securities and Exchange Commission in Washington and who thus, no doubt, had some good political contacts (such as Senator Lyndon B. Johnson). But Cook's impact upon the company has been in the marketing area—such as bringing industry into the region and selling electric heating in homes and buildings.

It is rare for a power utility to reach outside the industry and to bring in a new executive at a high level. For most utilities, with guaranteed rates of return set by state regulatory agencies, the area of most uncertainty is politics. This situation is well documented in a book by Senator Lee Metcalf, *Overcharge* (45), which is bitterly critical of the industry. A.E.P. seems to have taken a route other than politics in order to ensure survival and profitability. It has focused on more commonplace strategies, such as innovation, service, and marketing, rather than on political support; there is a marked contrast with aged, inefficient Con Ed, with its graybeards, emphasis upon tenure in the firm, and political alliances. Presumably, the internal structure and the technology of these companies also differ markedly. An alert researcher or management trainee would no doubt spot the difference immediately, even at the lower reaches of the organizations.

One final illustration of environmental system goals will indicate how the very existence, as well as the character, of an organization can depend upon how it regards its environment of competitors and regu-

lators.[3] The example concerns a modest-sized shipping firm, Isbrandtsen. The world of deep-water shipping is not governed by "sound
business practices and competition" so much as by an Alice-in-Wonder-
land logic. (Every business community departs more or less from sound
business practices and competition, but shipping, railroading, and a few
others do so to a grotesque degree.) The industry is a legalized international cartel with a giant subsidy from the federal government (in
1960, the subsidy was 60 percent of total operating costs). It enjoys the
best of both worlds. If insurance rates or wages go up, the government
pays the bill. If too much trade goes to foreign companies, the government will require that more imports and exports be shipped in "U.S.
bottoms." But it is not likely that too much trade will go to other
countries because the cartel is world-wide, through the "conference," an
international group which has the power to set rates and carve up
territories.

The only irritants in this situation are the non-conference ships,
which operate like hit-and-run pirates, trying to take business away from
the cartel. Their chances are slim, despite laws limiting retaliation by
the conference ships. The laws are simply not enforced, and there are
documented examples of illegal activity by the cartel. To attempt to stay
out of the cartel and survive is to court disaster. Isbrandtsen courted
disaster for several decades before it finally caved in, when its president,
Hans Isbrandtsen, died and his son took over.

Hans Isbrandtsen and his company made money—not much, but
enough to carry on the battle. Efficiency was their weapon in an industry where there was no incentive for it. They also took spectacular risks
in political matters, staying within the law but running blockades (e.g.,
Taiwan's blockade of mainland China), to the annoyance of the State
Department, suing the government for illegal practices, attacking the
Secretary of State in full-page ads, and the like. The U.S. government
refused to give them business or to sell them surplus ships, and finally
the Maritime Commission allowed a rate war to take place in the Pacific
that was directed solely at Isbrandtsen. The weapon was a complex of
rate changes and restrictions that was subsequently declared illegal by
the Supreme Court, but not until the damage was done and the firm
had left the Pacific. Goods were being shipped by Isbrandtsen and the
cartel at 80 percent below established rates. Isbrandtsen paid out more

[3] Covered in one of the most striking of *Fortune's* stories by a master in
this art, Richard Austin Smith (77).

simply to load and unload the cargo than it made in freight charges. During this rate war Hans Isbrandtsen died, and his son later agreed to join the cartel. The son applied for a government subsidy, which the government indicated it would be delighted to review.

The elder Isbrandtsen simply did not believe that cartels and subsidies were a way of doing business. Instead, he cut costs and modernized and ran what was probably the most efficient firm in the business. To understand this company, one has to understand its goal of surviving and prospering outside the protective umbrella created by a business-government alliance. It is possible, though there is no way of telling, that, to him, even survival, that ultimate system goal, would not have been worth the price.

Product Characteristic Goals

Two organizations may have identical output goals, such as making steel, but may nevertheless differ markedly in terms of their product goals or, more exactly, their goals regarding the characteristics of their products. Such characteristics are quality, quantity, type, cost, styling, availability, and so on. One often hears product goals mentioned in the following terms: "We don't go in for those kinds of fancy steels; we are only interested in producing the basic stuff that industry needs." Or, "We are the Cadillac of the steel industry—we produce the high-quality steels in small quantity and leave the easy stuff to the others." Two different product goals are being invoked here.

For other examples, consider these typical statements:

> "We thought of getting into that, and had the patents, but we sold them off; that is not our dish of tea."
> "We should never have gotten into this line; it is foreign to the rest of our operation, and we just don't have the experience or the skills."
> "If we start to turn this stuff out in quantity, now that we know how to make it, it is going to change the whole character of this company; we will become a production outfit, and our top R and D men will leave."
> "We engineer everything to death around here; by the time we get it on the market the others have sewed the market up. So what if our product is 10 percent better? It is two years too late. This kind of thing is all right if you are in aerospace, but not in our business."

Product-goal decisions are being invoked in these cases. Such goals become built into the company and denote a degree of specialization and distinctive competence that shapes the behavior of the organization.

The distinction between "producing" juveniles who have (hopefully) learned how to obey adults and those who have (hopefully) developed insight into their own characters and ways of dealing with things is a product-goal distinction. Part of the difference between Dick and Inland, the institutions we described in the second chapter, is in their product goals. (Dick also had a system goal of stability and little change, while Inland prized change and did not value stability.) Both sought to reform delinquents, but the characteristics of their products differed markedly.

As with other types of goals, decisions about product characteristics are not susceptible to handy slogans or rules-of-thumb. More than one company has found that it did not have the capability to go from low-volume, high-cost quality items to high-volume, low-cost standard items. The whole character of the company can change with such a shift, and unanalyzed or unknown competencies and market situations that were highly favorable can evaporate.

The Commitment to Product Goals

Product goals do not exist in all organizations; for some organizations it does not matter what is made or what is the quality, variety, or prestige of the item. For others, these considerations are very important, either for sentimental or ideological reasons or perhaps because it is sensed that a distinctive competence would be violated by changes in product characteristics. Indeed, the issue of distinctive competence— "what we are good at," "not our dish of tea," "right down our line"—is one of the most revealing aspects of an organization that one can find.

When an organization adopts a certain strategy with regard to product characteristics, or finds that it has such a strategy, a great number of interests become invested in this way of doing its job, and the strategy takes on the character of an independent, autonomous goal. For many organizations, this is the measure and cause of their success; such factors as capital investments, specialized skills, internal political balances, marketing information, and relationships with suppliers and customers all act to support this bent. The profitability and success of Eastern Airlines during Rickenbacker's reign was due to this clear focus on just what kinds of product goals would be sought (low-quality service) as well as the system goal of low-cost operation. But when the environment changes, the organization finds it hard to make the changes in every aspect of its being. Other organizations with different product goals, or no particular product goals at all, may be the ones to benefit. What was once an asset—a committed organization, finely tuned in all its parts to certain goals—becomes a liability. Let us consider some examples.

THE GREAT A & P

Until recently, the Great Atlantic and Pacific Tea Company had been the largest grocery chain in the nation; for as long as most people could remember it had been the most successful and profitable one as well (60). It had built up its commanding position by an emphasis upon foodstuffs of uniform and good quality, priced low to ensure high volume. Then consumer habits and tastes shifted, and other stores found that consumers also wanted non-food items in the stores. These stores found the higher markup on these items very attractive. According to the *Fortune* story in 1963, A & P had dabbled in items such as drugs, cosmetics, kitchenware, and nylons but "with extreme caution and considerable distaste." A divisional president expressed the attitude in this way: "I think our primary purpose is to sell food cheaply, and tangents tend to hurt the food operation. There is a higher profit margin on nonfoods, but it's *just not our business.*"

It was also "not their business" to engage in promotional devices such as Sunday openings, stamps, and loss leaders, except in unusual circumstances. The other chains were growing fast on these techniques. However, the 1963 *Fortune* article describes an imminent change in strategy. Three new executive vice-president positions were created for "younger men" to placate a board restive with low profits and aggressive competitors. The "younger" men were aged 51, 59, and 62; on the other hand, the chief executive officer was 73, and the president was 67. One of the new vice-presidents was Melvin Alldredge, who was quoted as saying that he thought A & P was slow to take on non-foods, and he was not against this new step. His own contribution had been an emphasis upon modernizing the stores by means of glamour and all sorts of conveniences. He had even experimented with a discount-house–supermarket combination, a revolutionary undertaking for A & P. There were, then, signs of change.

However, product goals are not easy to alter, and traditions die slowly. Five years later, the "Young Turk" who, like all top executives and much of management had spent his career in A & P, had revised his position. The occasion was another *Fortune* story, titled "Look Who's Become a Take-Over Target: A & P" (7). Its product goals had apparently not changed, and the situation was worsening. Yet Mr. Alldredge said: "Basically we're in the food business; we don't want or need to promote." The executive of another chain expressed the contrasting perspective: "We're in whatever it takes to bring them in and sell them."

Product versus System Goals in the Textile Industry

FORSTMANN AND PRODUCT IDENTIFICATION

What is only a small part of the dynamics of supermarket retailing—the willingness to sell whatever the customer might buy rather than to maintain product goals—appears to be a matter of almost life and death in the textile industry. This old, technologically backward industry, protected by high government tariffs, government subsidies upon subsidies, and complex two-price systems, is still the haven of strong product identification among the executives. Their attachment to fibers such as wool, cotton, or silk and their resistance to new synthetic fibers, was so strong in the early 1960s that, at a meeting of the Fashion Institute of Technology, an executive of one large textile company was hissed by "silk men" in the audience when they felt that their true love had been slurred (92). When the demand for long-established, high-quality goods evaporates, many old-line companies just fold in preference to adopting new fibers or cheap versions of the old fiber. This happened to the old Forstmann Woolen Company of New Jersey. They continued to turn out five-dollar-a-yard quality goods on 500 looms when the market would support the production of only 50 looms. Stricken by debt, they were taken over by J. P. Stevens, a company whose chairman said in 1963: "If the public wants straw, we'll weave straw. We're not wedded to any particular product or fiber."

This particular take-over is worth examining in a little more detail, for it nicely illustrates how a strictly fiscal goal of profit (a system goal) allows one to turn debts into assets (as we saw in the case of J. P. Lannan and the North Shore railway in the last chapter), whereas a product goal ("We're in the wool business," or "We are in the business of producing high-quality wool at a price that will provide us with a reasonable return on investment") would render such a strategy unacceptable or even unperceived. I do not pretend to fully understand the matter myself, so I will just quote from the *Fortune* article (92), whose author, Richard J. Whalen, presumably knows what he is talking about.

> Forstmann was acquired for 280,000 shares of Stevens' stock, which was selling at $23 a share at the time, and its assets were transferred to Stevens' records at book value. Stevens tried to operate Forstmann but soon concluded its old mills could not be run competitively and would have to be liquidated. In anticipation of losses involved in running out and selling the Forstmann mills, a reserve fund was created. The proceeds of the liquidation, plus the reserve, produced a cash flow of $11 million for Stevens. In effect Stevens realized $41 a share for its 280,000 shares of stock. "It took two years of hard work and a lot of explanation to the board," said Kenneth W. Fraser, Stevens' financial vice president, "but this deal enhanced our equity by $11 million."[4]

STEVENS AND INNOVATION

The company that was the purchaser, J. P. Stevens, was considered the most progressive of the many textile companies in the country, at least in 1963. Stevens invested about one-half of one percent of sales in research and development, whereas the textile-industry average was *one-tenth* of one percent of sales (for industry as a whole the rate is two percent). The company utilized large computer installations and applications. It pioneered glass fabrics and unwoven fabrics, is highly diversified in fabrics and markets, and was the first to move its plants south in large number. Stevens has made good money. It is also still operated by direct descendants of the founder; the management of the firm has passed from father to son in a direct line for over a century and a half. As *Fortune* notes, even the DuPonts have had to rely on an occasional son-in-law (92).

INDIAN HEAD AND PROFITS

In direct contrast, in many respects, is the equally successful Indian Head Mills company, which has somewhat different system goals, although this company, too, is not enticed by any particular product-characteristic goals (62). Indian Head Mills had been losing money badly, like most of the many modest-sized textile companies, when it

---

[4] Courtesy of *Fortune* Magazine, August 1963.

was acquired by Textron in an effort to put together an integrated textile empire. Textron failed and began to sell off its textile property. The trade name of Indian Head was worth a good deal, and it was bought by an enterprising "professional manager," James E. Robinson, a Harvard Business School graduate with no experience in textiles. He proceeded to run it strictly in terms of that bedrock tenet of capitalism: money must flow in the direction in which it will earn the greatest profit. He began by selling off a good deal of Indian Head property and then buying more declining mills and selling off parts or most of them. This is easy to do. Even today, there are nearly unlimited possibilities for buying textile companies that have problems and can be acquired at less than book value. The losses thus incurred can be used to great advantage for tax purposes, as was suggested in the case of J. P. Stevens. Furthermore, with an unsentimental eye and no commitments to any products, Robinson retained those parts of the companies that were making money—thread here, lace there. He was able to put together an unintegrated but highly profitable group of companies strongly entrenched in their specific and narrow fields.

It is remarkable just how profitable the venture was. The net return on invested capital was more than double that of the industry as a whole, and in 1960 it was almost 20 per cent. The stocks of eight of the ten leading publicly owned textile companies sold for less than book value; Indian Head stock sold for 2.7 times book value. The book value of a share went from $2.72 in 1954 to $60.00 in 1962. However, and this is the revealing figure, the company's *operating* profit in 1961 was only five percent of sales. Indicators such as return on invested capital and book value reflected something other than the company's ability to produce goods at a profit. One reason these indicators were so high was that from 1955 to 1959 the firm paid no federal income taxes at all, despite a high return on invested capital, and in 1961, when the return was 17.6 percent, it paid only a pittance in taxes. It was still carrying forward $1,400,000 of unused tax credits. Thus, its profitability was based largely on nonrecurring profits.

Fiscal sleight of hand? Paper profits? Not at all. These figures reflect the system goals of the company; it has no product goals. As expressed by the president, the goal is not to produce textiles, let alone to manufacture products of particular quality, variety, or novelty. Nor is growth the goal. According to the policy manual prepared by the president, "the objective of this company is to increase the intrinsic value of the common stock." *Fortune* (62) goes on:

The manual then explains that the company is in the business *not* "to grow bigger for the sake of size, nor to become more diversified, nor to make the most or best of anything, nor to provide jobs, have the most modern plants, the happiest customers, lead in new product development, or to achieve any other status which has no relationship to the economic use of capital.

"Any or all of these may be, from time to time, a means to our objective, but means and ends must never be confused. Indian Head Mills is in business solely to improve the inherent value of the common stockholders' equity in the company."

The list of things for which the company is *not* in business is fairly representative of the variety of goals that companies can pursue: growth, diversification, quality, employment, technological advance, happy customers, and new products. But Indian Head is not even in business to make money out of production of goods. Its sole aim is to increase the value of the stock.

"We have no emotional involvement in the textile industry. We're in it through happenstance," said Robinson in 1961. Other members of the textile industry both on the business and labor side have assailed this philosophy. According to the *Fortune* article:

They complained that Robinson does not try to save some of these situations by putting money into mechanization and automation in order to cut costs. A top official of one of the oldest and largest U.S. textiles companies asked bitterly, "Is he trying to build up a textile business or just to make money?" Told of the comment, Robinson replied, "He has the money. I don't have three generations of accumulated capital with which to protect the status quo."[5]

What have been the consequences of Indian Head Mills' goal? We have already noted the dramatic increase in the value of common stock and the very substantial dividends paid out to stockholders. In addition, however, Robinson was hung in effigy in at least one textile town whose major source of employment was closed down. Also, many plants both in

[5] Courtesy of *Fortune* Magazine, May 1962.

New England and in the South were closed, with resulting dislocation of labor and local economic problems. Viewed abstractly, on the broad macroeconomic plane of capitalism, there is a good deal of force in Robinson's logic. Money should go where it will earn the greatest profit.

Thus, Robinson would disagree on a number of points with the leadership of J. P. Stevens, which is also very successful. Robinson believes in the elimination of subsidies and tariffs in the textile industry on the ground that the industry needs to be thoroughly shaken up before it can become healthy, whereas Stevens has led the trek to Washington for tariffs and subsidies. Robinson feels the answer to industry problems lies in neither mechanization nor automation because such steps merely increase the glut of goods in an oversupplied market and lower the price. But Stevens is a leader in mechanization, automation, R and D, and high-volume production. Indian Head rarely invests in new equipment or attempts to improve efficiency in the firms it buys, but simply writes off the inefficient segments, leaving the rest as they are. In contrast, Stevens, which has itself made quite a few acquisitions, invests further in their improvement.

SUMMARY

It has been shown that at least three stances may be taken in the textile industry:

(1) Firms may emphasize product goals, whereby they specialize in fibers and in degrees of quality and quantity; these are the traditional firms concerned with "building up a textile business." In other industries, which are not beset with the peculiar, endemic, and long-standing problems of the textile industry, such a stance is often profitable and applauded.

(2) Companies can take a market approach, emphasizing system goals of efficiency, innovation, diversification, and growth, as found in J. P. Stevens, where they would weave straw if that was what was wanted. This is the current ideal of most progressive businesses.

(3) Businesses can adopt a system goal favored by investors, stressing only the return on capital. This approach reflects the unreconstructed view, stemming from traditional capitalistic dogma, that return on invested capital is the only

goal a firm may be justified in pursuing; other problems will be solved through the automatic play of competition within the industry and between industries.

Whatever one wishes to dub these three positions—goals, strategies, or something else—it is clear that they reflect quite different views concerning the direction in which companies should be moving and what the ideal company would look like. It is also clear that any researcher, consultant, or manager should be aware of these differences. For example, the ideal middle or upper-middle manager for the various types of firms would be quite different. In the first type, he should be aware of the traditions of the industry, loyal to his product and his company, and blessed with a sense of all the intricacies of producing and marketing the firm's particular products. His loyalty to the company must be particularistic—based on its specific characteristics. He is like a craftsman—a "wool" man first and an employee of a particular company second—but loyal to both. In the second type of company, the perfect manager is the model of the business-school graduate, aware not only of the latest techniques of problem analysis and cost cutting, but of the risks and promise of long-range research and development, capital investment, market coverage, and consumer shifts. His loyalty is to his skills, which are transferable from company to company; indeed, he may seek such varied experience to increase his value to any one company. He is preoccupied with the production and marketing of whatever will sell, and he believes his role is to increase the efficient use of society's resources, given the absolute power of the customer. In the third kind of company the ideal manager is the unsentimental slide-rule type who calculates only in terms of investment and return and the stock market values. He is loyal neither to the product, nor to his specific skills, nor to the company, but only to the setting in which he can have the greatest impact. He is preoccupied with the intangibles of the capital structure of an industry and its evaluation by investors, rather than with the problems of producing wool or the efficient use of tangible resources of capital, land, and labor.

Quality as a Product Goal

One of the most common examples of product-characteristic goals that shape an organization concerns the degree of attention to quality. All organizations proclaim their aim to be quality goods or services, but what is generally meant is the degree of quality necessary to prevent a decline in sales or customer acceptance. When we discuss quality as a goal, however, we are speaking of those organizations that attempt to provide goods or services whose quality exceeds that of competitors, or, in some cases, quality higher than the minimum demanded by controlling agencies, such as legislators. Quality becomes a problem at Ford Motor Company only when it appears to dip below the standards of its competitors. For Daimler-Benz, the makers of Mercedes cars, quality is a goal in itself. That company has infinitely higher quality standards than Detroit or the mass producers in Europe.

Organizations which are known for the quality of their goods or services appear to have certain characteristics in common. They draw upon a special pool of labor skills and management talent or have a long history of employing talented people. They are conscious of their quality, pride themselves on it, talk about it a good deal, and often sacrifice short-run gains to maintain this goal. They cater to a select segment of the market—an upper-class neighborhood, in the case of schools; middle-class clients, in the case of welfare agencies; well-to-do customers, for business firms; or, in the case of industrial firms, customers that supply products to highly technical, specialized, and often government-related operations. These characteristics are not produced overnight in an organization or upon the stern warnings of an executive; it is difficult to move from a low-quality product to a high-quality product.

The case of Gar Wood industries illustrates how difficult it also is to move in the reverse direction, from high to low quality. After having produced high-quality custom boats, Gar Wood decided to compete with Chris Craft in the market for cheap, mass-produced boats. It found that it could not induce its workers to shift over to the new techniques and lower quality standards. The company finally had to give up production of the new lines at the base plant and build a new one in a location many miles away, hiring new people. Quality had been built into the old producing organization, and the shift in goals required a new organization with new people (68, pp. 53–54).

Another instance is this unverified story from a businessman who was tangentially involved. During World War II the government required, in very large quantities, a timing device for exploding artillery shells. Bids were requested. A highly respected, well-known watch company studied the specifications in detail, the engineers outlined a production process, and the government was quoted a price. Meanwhile, however, an upstart in the field, Timex, also examined the specifications and made a bid. It was a great deal lower than the other bids. What had happened was that in their preoccupation with quality, the long-established watch manufacturer had designed the part and the production process as the company was wont to do for extremely accurate, long-lasting precision watches. It could not, in a sense, do otherwise. This was what the organization was geared to. Timex, however, looked at the problem as a simple engineering job, without the precedents built up over the years in traditional watch firms. Timex quality was sufficient for the task at hand, and they were awarded the contract. Timex watches, indeed, are designed and built upon this basis, on the theory that most people do not need a high degree of accuracy and that the cost of annual cleaning is so high that users will be prepared to buy a new watch after it has run out its short life. Their watch designs are simplified, thus enabling them to use cheap unskilled labor in southern plants for mass production.

A glimpse of an organization with a product goal of quality is provided by the *Fortune* story of "Daimler-Benz: Quality über Alles" (70). The firm built the world's first practical automobile and has been building quality cars in small numbers for over 75 years. The chief engineer of the company described the 75-year-old tradition as "constant experimentation, concentration on new developments, and continuous improvement." This has meant that the Mercedes has incorporated, as standard equipment, all significant innovations as soon as they appear, whether the public demands them or not and without regard to the increase in the cost of the car. For example, Daimler-Benz introduced such innovations as four-wheel suspension, fuel injection, and joint rear swing axle long before they were adopted by other manufacturers. The company is dominated by engineers and has an adequate pool of skilled labor. Its workers have lived and worked for generations in the German towns where the cars are produced, and they take a fierce pride in their skilled craftsmanship.

American car makers begin with what they think the public wants in terms of appearance, size, features, power, and price, based upon extensive marketing research and the whims of a few top people. With frequent styling changes mistakes can be adjusted, and popular models can be imitated. The manufacturers are also in a position to manipulate customer desires to some extent, through advertising. This is the familiar strategy of high-volume, mass-market enterprises, whether for cars or for grocery stores. Daimler-Benz has always built automobiles to the tastes of the engineers whether the public likes it or not. As *Fortune* (70) puts it:

> With an almost charming arrogance, Daimler-Benz engineers explain it is unreasonable to expect that the average customer, or any given number of customers, would know what it takes to fulfill the requirements of safety, comfort, economy, performance, and durability in an automobile. It is the automobile builder's business to know and conscientiously to satisfy those requirements, and thus fashion a car that is in the best interest of all customers. As for the looks of the car, it should be understood that a Mercedes is built from the inside out. After the interior has been meticulously designed for the proper headroom, legroom, visibility, etc., the exterior, as the engineers put it, follows naturally as "an envelope or mantle for the functions of the car," and its beauty "speaks through the form itself and not through exaggerated ornamentation."[6]

The public has always liked the Daimler-Benz product, even though output has been miniscule compared to that of American firms. In 1960 the company sold barely over 120,000 passenger cars in the world-wide market. Even so, this was a jump of 100 percent over the 1955 output. Such a firm constitutes a very attractive target for a takeover. Capitalizing upon the name and reputation, it would be possible to institute mass production of inferior cars, and it might take a few years before the public became aware of the drop in quality. At the time of the *Fortune* article, just such a danger had presented itself; the firm had been quietly taken over by Ruhr industrialists after they had finished serving their war-crime sentences, and it was merged with another firm which produced the small, cheap BKW auto. The engineers at Daimler-Benz were worried.

Not all firms which emphasize high quality need be small operations with highly skilled craftsmen. Magnavox has produced TV sets, radios, and hi-fi sound systems for years on a volume basis, while competing most successfully with the giants in the field (7). Here again a decision was made to emphasize product quality, and the marketing and production aspects were made to conform to that decision. While

[6] Courtesy of *Fortune* Magazine, August 1961.

sales in the consumer electronic industry were standing still from about 1958 to 1963, Magnavox sales nearly doubled (to 200 million dollars in 1962). In 1963 it led in many areas (stereo hi-fi phonographs, big-screen TV sets, and combinations). Its return on invested capital was a neat 26.5 percent in 1962—only eight of the 500 largest industrial corporations had a higher return. Magnavox managed all this by selling only "big-ticket" (high-priced), high-quality products through franchised dealers at an absolutely firm price. Zenith, for example, had about 30,000 retailers in 1963; Magnavox had no middlemen and only 2,200 dealers—in the best department and music stores, strategically located around the country. Discount sales are endemic to the industry, but unheard of for Magnavox. The company does little innovating, but waits for others to develop long-play records, stereo, and color TV. However, it is insistent on quality.

Incidentally, Magnavox violates many prescriptions of progressive management as well. It is run single-handedly by a perfectionist president, who is the largest stockholder (eight percent), with a very small administrative staff, no committees, and a small executive team that he brought in from the outside. "I have not had the time or patience to develop management," the president admits. There is no emphasis upon growth *per se,* and only with a great deal of reluctance did the company "compromise" itself by introducing a low-priced "second set." A salesman, the president said, would be a fool to push it when he can make much more on the higher priced sets. An inexpensive phonograph was developed, only to be junked by the president when he heard its tone. An emphasis upon high quality need not be associated with one-man rule, but perhaps it helps when high volume is involved.

Derived Goals

Finally, let us at least mention a somewhat residual category, one rarely dealt with explicitly in these terms, but of great importance for understanding organization—derived goals. We tend to forget, or neglect, the fact that organizations have an enormous potential for affecting the lives of all who come into contact with them. They control or can activate a multitude of resources, not just land and machinery and employees, but police, governments, communications, art, and other areas, too. That is, an organization, as a legally constituted entity, can ask for police protection and public prosecution, can sue, and can hire a private police force with considerably wider latitude and power than an individual can command. It can ask the courts to respond to requests and to make legal rulings. It can petition for changes in other areas of government—zoning laws, fair-trade laws, consumer labeling, and protection and health laws. It determines the content of advertising, the art work in its products and packages, the shape and color of its buildings. It can move out of a community, and it selects the communities in which it will build. It can invest in times of imminent recession or it can retrench; support or fight government economic policies or fair employment practices. In short, organizations generate a great deal of power that may be used in a way not directly related to producing goods and services or to survival. Presumably, organizations need most of these powers to function, but there is also a great deal of latitude in how the power is exercised.

We explored many of these issues at the end of the last chapter, when we spoke of the organization's impact upon its environment. They are discussed to some extent in books and courses dealing with the "social responsibilities" of business and businessmen. These issues also constitute a topic which is appended to the business-school training program with little enthusiasm, many generalities and much oracular moralism. The whole question deserves better, not only because economic organizations have an enormous impact upon our society, but because derived goals become embedded in organizations and should be closely examined if we wish to understand organizations. Neither the simplicities of the radical left nor the mushy self-congratulation of the business community will suffice. But if these two have failed us in understanding how power is utilized, so has the social scientist. Organizational analysis has been wary of dealing with organizational goals in general, let alone with the subtle, submerged, and latent area of derived goals.

Goals and Organizational Character

I have paid so much attention, and devoted so many pages, to the neglected area of goals because I believe that they provide a key, not found elsewhere, to an organization's "character," and thus to its behavior. The concept of technology can tell us much; the examination of structure can tell us more. But goals are, to some unknown but perhaps substantial degree, independent of these factors. At the least, they provide a quick conceptual entry to the organization. Finally, they reflect more readily the uniqueness of organizations and the role of specific influences within the more general technological and structural categories. For goals are the product of a variety of influences, some of them enduring and some fairly transient. To enumerate some of these influences: the personality of top executives, the history of the organization, its community environment, the norms and values of the other organizations with which it deals (e.g., the "mentality of the steel industry"), the technology and structure of the organization, and ultimately the cultural setting.

Few organizations, like few individuals, have peripheral vision, enabling them to single out and accurately assess all the events that might be important to them. Some successful organizations, like some successful individuals, have tunnel vision—they see only in one direction, and they see a narrow bit of the world at that. The range of vision can be altered. Expanding a sales department into a marketing department and conducting market surveys and systematic studies of competitors' behavior is a way of broadening vision. Some other ways include diversifying the board of directors, recruiting middle and upper management from other industries, doing basic research, and participating in trade associations. But only to a limited extent can the organization rely upon these techniques, for even with expanded vision the goals of the organization still provide highlights and blinders. Montgomery Ward did not "see" the extent of the move to the suburbs (Sears did), not because of faulty intelligence information, but because the diversification and investment that would be required with suburban stores was incompatible with fiscal beliefs and centralized authority (or was thought to be). A & P did not miss the obvious shift in consumer preferences because no one observed what the competition was doing, but because such a change in strategy would have meant a threatening change in management expertise and the need to introduce new people. A & P's goal was not to adjust to such changes, but to do what the company could do well: sell food in a straightforward manner at very low margins. (Actually, the situation was more complicated. A & P is also a substantial *producer* of foods, thus reinforcing its concern with high-volume food items; major investments, and thus much organizational power, lay in the production side of the business.)

Goals become built into organizations, making change difficult. Personnel at all levels construct their organizational life around the reality of goals. Elaborate checks and balances can be constructed where risks are not favored, and these become justifications or, mistakenly, explanations for caution. Where risks are expected, the decision-making machinery is simplified and communication lines are direct and multiple; but when operations are conducted this way, it is difficult to ensure adequate analysis even when it is desired. Personnel who cannot adapt to the prevailing goals leave or find their advancement blocked; those who do adapt recruit others of similar views. Technical people are recruited for work on specific products, limiting the company's ability to shift to other markets. It is easier to buy a company in a different market than to break into it. In a sense, "people" do not resist change but, rather, patterns of interaction, relationships, bargains, negotiations, mutual adjustments, and, above all, forms of solutions or ways of handling problems resist change. The concept of goals, or organizational character, directs us to these types of formulations rather than to those relating to techniques or training.

Goals, in this sense, are necessary for concerted effort. It is possible for an organization to lack important goals, or to lack a distinctive character. Without firm goals, such organizations are subject to vagrant pressures from within and without, even as they may grow and prosper. There is, of course, a direction of effort, but it may be changeable, vulnerable, and not firmly anchored in the organizational structure. While this gives the organization flexibility, it also provides few resources for unusual effort of a concerted kind. Organizations are tools; system, product, and derived goals shape the form of the tool, indicating for what it can or cannot be used. An organization with weakly held goals is a poor tool for accomplishing ends, so that it may be shaped by opportunistic forces in the environment (68, pp. 74–75). Thus, goals represent a positive resource to organizations.

This is not to say that all goals are "good" or desirable; some may bring about the decline or demise of the organization, as we have seen in a number of instances (Isbrandtsen, A & P, Endicott, Forstmann). Generally, their goals were adequate in a different environment, but they did not change in time. Indeed, the problem is often that the past appropriateness of goals prevents executives from seeing their present inappropriateness.

Finally, it is clear that goals are multiple and conflicting, and thus the "character" of an organization is never stable. We have emphasized dramatic examples of goals and have generally singled out only one in a particular organization. But organizations pursue a variety of goals, sometimes in sequence, sometimes simultaneously. DuPont, for example, is both innovative and conservative; it is large enough to emphasize quality in some areas and quantity in others. At times these aims conflict, at other times the conflicting goals can be segregated, just as we have seen that organizations may include varying structures and technologies. It would even appear that tension among conflicting goals can be as healthy for an organization as the differentiation of subunits. Despite inevitable costs, such tension helps insure ready channels for changes in goals, when appropriate (93).

We began this book by stressing the variety of organizational forms that exist and emphasizing that there is no one best way to run organizations. We have looked at varying technologies, structures, and leadership styles, and different means of relating to the environment. To all this we can now add that goals also vary and that "successful" organizations do not have identical goals. The *Fortune* profiles—the best single source of general material on specific organizations—illustrate the variety of goals that can be pursued by successful organizations. Presumably a complex society that values a plurality of means and ends will depend upon a variety of organizations that differ in their technologies, structures, and goals. For any one organization, the problem is to insure that technology, structure, and goals are in harmony. This is what good management or good leadership is all about.

Summary
and Conclusions

Structure, technology, environment, goals—these are the concepts that have been stressed in this book. Leadership, interpersonal relations, morale, productivity—these concepts have not been stressed. The difference is one of perspective. In this book we have sought to redress the balance between the social-psychological and the structural perspectives, between studies of parts of organizations and conceptions of the whole, between concern with productivity and other managerial values and concern with community and societal values. Our perspective is not meant to supplant other perspectives; it all depends upon what the student of organizations wants to consider or to accomplish. But, obviously, we believe that if organizations are to be studied, rather than individuals or group processes, then the structural view, characteristic of sociology, is superior. Furthermore, we believe that the structural view provides a more economical approach to organizational change and problem solving. There are several reasons for this conviction.

One may attempt to change an individual's personality and attitudes in the hope or expectation that the result will be changes in behavior. But this is difficult to accomplish, especially in organizations. We have few proven techniques, they are expensive, and we know that relapses to old ways are common. Training in human-relations skills, injunctions to "delegate" or to be sensitive to human needs do no harm; in some organizations where conditions are truly poor, they may do quite a bit of good. But most organizations and most of the people involved in them are aware of the value of common decency and of what Hertzberg, Mausner, and Snyderman call "hygienic supervision"

(28). Attempts to change personality and attitudes can go only so far and, besides, they are costly.

However, there is enormous potential in organizations for a direct attack on behavior, without intermediate efforts to alter attitudes or personality. It is possible to control the reward structure (in particular, the kind of behavior that receives positive rewards); the stimuli or signals that are presented to the individual and that trigger his response; the rules under which he is forced to operate; and the perception of just what is valued in the organization by means of strategies such as the route to the top or emphasis on stability or change, volume or quality. This enormous potential for changing behavior can be utilized without substantial outside resources or time taken from productive activity, without invasion of privacy, and without discontinuity between what is preached and what is actually allowed to be practiced. Designing and managing the structure of the organization is the key. Behavior evoked by such devices as rules, role prescriptions, reward structures, and lines of communication is reinforced daily and becomes part of the stable expectations of employees. It is possible to design jobs, or roles, for the average person (assuming a given level of training and experience) rather than to expect an individual to have superhuman qualities to fill an impossible role.

In the first chapter we examined several typical instances of mistaken analysis of organizational problems; in each of these cases, the characteristics of individuals were wrongly held to be the main source of the problem. We asserted that the structure of the various organizations was actually faulty. Supposedly, the correctional institution was custodial because of the low quality of its guards and their custodial attitudes. The vice-president of production was presumably to blame because he did not delegate authority. The plant manager was incompetent and had to be told what to do by the central headquarters. We argued that the attitudes and behavioral dispositions of the guards were once treatment-oriented, but that after working in the institution they had become custodial. The rules, structure, and techniques of the institution had changed their attitudes and behavior, despite its training program and the official treatment-oriented goals. The problems of the vice-president stemmed from the sales-dominated structure of the organization at a time when the power of production should have been increasing because of new product lines. The failure of the plant manager and the success of his replacement were due at least as much to the presence of extensive initial interference from headquarters and the withdrawal of that interference when the replacement arrived. Of course, there are incompetent managers, and workers are sometimes not all that one would like them to be. But the immediate resort to explanations in terms of personality or human relations is not warranted; the first question to be asked is whether the structure of the organization, or unit, or role, is the appropriate one for the tasks being demanded. Even if the structure is appropriate, it can be adjusted somewhat to compensate for particular human qualities. Failing such an adjustment, it may be necessary to be reconciled to failure to reach a goal or to find a new vice-president or plant manager. But these alternatives should be the last resort, not the first.

The discussion in the first chapter thus raised the question: what are the different kinds of structures and what are the different kinds of tasks? These problems were considered in Chapters Two and Three. All practitioners contend that no two organizations are alike. Each insists that his organization is unique—indeed, even more unique than all other unique organizations. On the other hand, in the quest for basic laws many social scientists stress the similarity of organizations, seeking ever more general (and ever more unenlightening) statements about such matters as leadership, morale, and the nature of organizations. The current fad is to inventory basic propositions which will hold for all or most organizations. Both views are correct in a literal sense, since organizations are all unique and they all have some things in common; but both propositions are profoundly wrong in a strategic sense.

Regarding the first proposition, all organizations, like all people and all organs and all cells, are indeed unique. But there are enough systematic differences, and systematic similarities, to allow us to generalize. Otherwise it would be impossible to use such terms as organizations, people, and cells. Without these generalizations, it would even be impossible for organizations to exist; organizations are based upon the assumption that an acceptable degree of standardization is possible, despite the irreducible uniqueness. What we must discover are *patterns* of variation, which hold despite the uniqueness of markets, structure, personnel, history, and environment and which provide fairly distinct types that can be used for analysis and prediction. We must also discover the patterns that do obtain in market situations, structure, and the rest. To the manager, his organization is unique; but only by comparing it with the experience of other organizations can he learn much about it, and to do this he must generalize.

Regarding the second proposition, all organizations do have basic similarities. But to know this is to know less than we need to know today to understand, change, rule, or control organizations. Our need for sophistication in this immensely organizational society goes beyond the simple ability to observe organizations as if we had just arrived from Mars or the Middle Ages. That organizations differ must be our pre-occupation today. In Chapter Two, we contrasted a custodially oriented and a treatment-oriented correctional institution and a routine rayon mill and a nonroutine electronics company to drive home the point that their structures differed, for good and legitimate reasons. In fact, we made the point that the custodial institution and the rayon mill had more in common with each other than they did with the treatment-oriented institution and the electronics company, and vice versa. On the other hand, what was common to the two correctional institutions, or to the two business firms, was not enlightening. What worked for one institution or firm would not work for the other.

But that wasn't saying too much. The differences were clear, but what could we do with a simple distinction based upon the degree to which tasks were routine or nonroutine? Obviously, such a distinction was too crude to deal with the variety of organizational types we assume to exist. We needed a better understanding of this simple contrast and a better understanding of the occasions for highly structured organizations and for those with fluid, amorphous structures. We postponed the first problem—a better understanding of the contrast—to take up the second. Since highly structured organizations are generally called bureaucratic, and bureaucracy is a dirty word, in the first part of Chapter Three we were obliged to explore the occasion for bureaucracy or structure.

We did not find the source of bureaucracy in nervous, insecure, petty officials bent on protecting the *status quo* at all odds or on maxi-mizing their individual power. Nor did we find the occasion for less bureaucratic ("nonbureaucratic," as we called it) organizations to be the spirit of democracy, individual autonomy, good human relations, and fearless frontiersmanship. Instead, we argued that the bureaucratic form results from a successful attempt to do what all organizations seek to accomplish—to minimize the impact of extra-organizational influences upon members; to promote a high degree of specialization to ensure efficiency and competency; and to control as much as possible the uncer-tainties and variabilities of the environment.

But where the environment changes too rapidly to be controlled or compensated for, and where tasks are too ill-defined or too variable to permit maximum specialization, a high degree of bureaucracy or structure is not possible. Instead, it is necessary to risk the intrusion of extra-organizational influences while trying to minimize them through the expensive device of professionalization of personnel. The advantages of specialization are lost in order to promote flexibility and problem solving. The portals and orifices of the organization cannot be sealed off to ensure stability and predictability; instead, the environment must be allowed inside, to ensure adaptability. While the cost will be great, the selling price of the goods or services will be correspondingly higher. But, we argued, the thrust in organizations is toward routinization, standardization, and bureaucracy. This trend is inherent in the nature of an industrial civilization, even though the wealth created by the efficiency and productive force of large bureaucratic organizations lets us afford the affluence of customized, unique, and expensive missiles, Mercedes, and psychoanalysts.

Having thus defended bureaucracy and structure, we were free to leave the routine-nonroutine, or bureaucratic-nonbureaucratic, distinction in order to look at more complex models and problems. For example, some parts of large organizations are fairly routine (such as production) and others are fairly nonroutine (engineering or R and D). Rather than to reduce the difference, we saw from one study that it was advantageous to maximize it; the appropriate techniques are used to help them work together. We explored a more elaborate typology of organizations, based upon a close analysis of two aspects of routineness and two aspects of nonroutineness, which could vary independently. This produced a fourfold typology, with the types labeled craft, nonroutine, engineering, and routine. We applied this analysis, as before, to both economic and nonprofit organizations, and argued that a management style which is successful in one situation cannot be imported to another situation without extensive modification. We also argued that most of the vaunted solutions to organizational problems peddled by consulting firms and the social sciences are limited to only certain kinds of organizations. If you can choose the one which fits your technology and structure, well and good. This analysis led to the conclusion that it is essential to have the ability to analyze technology and structure; the fourfold classification, and another one based upon three types of firms, were meant to provide some assistance along these lines.

These findings marked the conclusion of our analysis of the strictly internal affairs of organizations. We omitted a great deal which interests the sociologist, such as the role of the foreman, leadership techniques, communication channels, the nature of authority, the effects of size, union-management relations, and industrial conflict. Many of these matters are also the province of other disciplines, and the reasonably well-read student will pick them up.

But he will not pick up much regarding two complex but fascinating areas that even the sociologist has been negligent in exploring: the environment and organizational goals. The aim of Chapter Four, dealing with the environment, was modest—to alert the student to some of the many influences that impinge on and shape organizations. One group of factors concerned such general and miscellaneous aspects of the environment as time perspectives, organizational legitimacy, cooptation, regional and cultural influences, and cultural beliefs regarding pigeons. The other set of influences concerned relations with other organizations; from this frame of reference we examined the extent of reciprocity among organizations and the "willing suspension of competition." We ignored such subjects as price-fixing, cartels, and espionage, since the average manager is insulated from these decisions; instead, we focused upon seemingly irrational or inefficient practices that have their justification and explanation in environmental relationships of a subtle kind. Finally, we took a brief look at business and politics, reinforcing the point that organizations constitute the environment for other groups in society, as well as the other way around.

Organizations are tools designed to achieve various goals. To understand them fully, one must understand the goals they pursue. Despite complex conceptual and definitional problems in this area, which may be one reason why even sociologists have shied away from it, we felt it was instructive to make the attempt. In Chapter Five we held that goals are multiple, conflicting, pursued in sequence, open to group bargaining, and, in general, problematical, rather than obvious and given. Not only are they not obvious and given, but they provide the best single clue to the distinctive "character" of an organization. For both the social scientist and this management trainee, the most complete understanding of an organization will come through an analysis of its goals and basic strategies.

We began with a discussion of the possible differences between the goals of large investors and those of managers or of the rest of the organization. Then we singled out four types of goals for illustrative analysis, drawing heavily upon the "corporation stories" of *Fortune* magazine—a mine of fascinating data on the existing variety of organizational goals and strategies. These four types were output, system, product, and derived goals. Throughout, we were concerned, as always, to convey the diversity of organizational life—there is no one goal for business firms; there is no one best strategy—and yet to indicate that the diversity has a pattern. Certain recurring choices must be made; probably some basic forms of strategy can be chosen. We were not successful in laying out a clear pattern, nor did we attempt to link goals to structure and technology. Such sophistication, if possible at all, will take some time to achieve.

The chapters on environment and goals were meant to flush the student out from his preoccupation with the firm, narrow technology of internal management into the mushy, but richer and fecund, marshes of statesmanship and strategies. While we were not explicit about the matter of statesmanship, we obviously agree with Philip Selznick, who has written the most cogent essay in this area (69). The technician who rules a large organization is not likely to be aware of the enormous scope of the power inherent in organizational activity. We hold that it is vital to our society for the organizational leader to transcend the technology of administration and to focus upon such matters as organizational mission and character and the responsiveness of the inevitably bureaucratic, authoritarian organization to a presumably democratic society (59).

references

1. Belknap, I., and Steinle, J. G. *The community and its hospitals.* Syracuse, N.Y.: Syracuse Univ. Press, 1963.
2. Bendix, R. *Work and authority in industry.* New York: Wiley, 1956.
3. Bennis, W. *Changing organizations.* New York: McGraw-Hill, 1966.
4. Berle, A. A., and Means, G. C. *The modern corporation and private property.* New York: Macmillan, 1932.
5. Blau, P. M., Hydebrand, W. V., and Stauffer, R. E. The structure of small bureaucracies. *Amer. Sociol. Rev.,* 1966, *31,* 179–191.
6. Blauner, R. *Alienation and freedom: The factory worker and his industry.* Chicago: Univ. of Chicago Press, 1964.
7. Brown, S. H. Magnavox goes its own golden way. *Fortune,* 1964 (Feb.).
8. Brown, S. H. Look who's become a take-over target: A & P. *Fortune,* 1968 (Sept.).
9. Brown, W. *Explorations in management.* London: Heinemann, 1960.
10. Burns, T., and Stalker, G. M. *The management of innovation.* London: Tavistock, 1961.
11. Cordtz, D. There's another generation of whiz kids at Ford. *Fortune,* 1967 (Jan.).
12. Cottrell, W. F. Of time and the railroader. *Amer. Sociol. Rev.,* 1939, *4,* 190–198. Available in the Bobbs-Merrill Reprint Series, No. 8–54.
13. Crozier, M. *The bureaucratic phenomenon.* Chicago: Univ. of Chicago Press. 1964.
14. Cumming, W. W. A bird's eye glimpse of men and machines. In Ulrich, R., Stachnik, T., and Mabry, J. (Eds.), *Control of human behavior.* Chicago: Scott, Foresman, 1966.
15. Cyert, R., and March, J. *A behavioral theory of the firm.* Englewood Cliffs, N.J.: Prentice-Hall, 1963.
16. Deutscher, I. Words and deeds: Social science and social policy. *Social Probl.,* 1966, *13,* 235–254.
17. Domhoff, W. *Who rules America?* Englewood Cliffs, N.J.: Prentice-Hall, 1967.
18. Durkheim, E. *The division of labor in society.* Trans. by G. Simpson. New York: The Free Press, 1949. First published in French in 1893.

19. Edelman, M. *The symbolic uses of politics.* Urbana, Ill.: Univ. of Illinois Press, 1967.

20. Epstein, E. *The corporation in American politics.* Englewood Cliffs, N.J.: Prentice-Hall, 1969.

21. Galbraith, J. K. *The new industrial state.* Boston: Houghton Mifflin, 1967.

22. Gordon, R. A. *Business leadership in the large corporation.* Berkeley, Calif.: Univ. of California Press, 1961. First published in 1945.

23. Gouldner, A. W. *Patterns of industrial bureaucracy.* New York: The Free Press, 1954.

24. Granick, D. *The European executive.* New York: Doubleday, 1962.

25. Guest. R. *Organizational change.* Homewood, Ill.: Dorsey Press, 1962.

26. Harrington, M. *Toward a democratic left.* New York: Macmillan, 1968.

27. Harris, R. *The real voice.* New York: Macmillan, 1964.

28. Hertzberg, F., Mausner, B., and Snyderman, B. *The motivation to work.* New York: Wiley, 1960.

29. Horowitz, D., and Erlich, R. Big brother as a holding company. *Ramparts,* 1968 (Nov. 30, Dec. 14, and Dec. 28).

30. Janowitz, M. *The professional soldier.* New York: The Free Press, 1960.

31. Jaques, E. *The measurement of responsibility.* Cambridge, Mass.: Harvard Univ. Press, 1956.

32. Kaufman. H. *The forest ranger: A study in administrative behavior.* Baltimore: The Johns Hopkins Press, 1960.

33. Kay, H. We're the most enterprising utility in this country. *Fortune,* 1964 (May).

34. Kerr, C., and Siegel, A. The interindustry propensity to strike—An international comparison. In Kornhauser, A., Dubin, R., and Ross, A. M. (Eds.), *Industrial conflict.* New York: McGraw-Hill, 1954.

35. Lasch, C. *The new radicalism in America.* New York: Knopf, 1965.

36. Lawrence, P. R., and Lorsch, J. W. *Organization and environment.* Cambridge, Mass.: Harvard Univ. Press, 1967.

37. Likert, R. *New patterns of management.* New York: McGraw-Hill, 1961.

38. Likert, R. *The human organization.* New York: McGraw-Hill, 1967.

39. Mahoney, S. What happened at Endicott Johnson after the band stopped playing. *Fortune,* 1962 (Sept.).

40. Mann, F. C. Towards an understanding of the leadership role in formal organizations. In Dubin, R., Homans, G. C., Mann, F. C.,

and Miller, D. C., *Leadership and productivity*. San Francisco: Chandler, 1965.

41. March, J., and Simon, H. *Organizations*. New York: Wiley, 1958.
42. Massie, J. L. Management theory. In March, J. (Ed.), *The handbook of organizations*. Chicago: Rand McNally, 1965.
43. McCreary, E., Jr., and Guzzardi, W., Jr. Reciprocity: A customer is a company's best friend. *Fortune*, 1965 (June).
44. McGregor, D. *The professional manager*. New York: McGraw-Hill, 1967.
45. Metcalf, L., and Reihemer, V. *Overcharge*. New York: McKay, 1967.
46. Meyers, H. B. A hell of a different way to run a railroad. *Fortune*, 1963 (Sept.).
47. Meyers, H. B. The sweet, secret world of Forrest Mars. *Fortune*, 1967 (May).
48. Miller, W. B. Interinstitutional conflict as a major impediment to delinquency prevention. *Hum. Organization*, 1958, *17*, 20–23.
49. Mintz, M. *By prescription only*. Boston: Beacon Press, 1967.
50. Nader, R. *Unsafe at any speed*. New York: Grossman, 1965.
51. O'Hanlon, T. Con Edison: The company you love to hate. *Fortune*, 1966 (March).
52. Parsons, T. *Structure and process in modern societies*. New York: The Free Press, 1960.
53. Perrow, C. The analysis of goals in complex organizations. *Amer. Sociol. Rev.*, 1961, *26*, 859–866.
54. Perrow, C. Organizational prestige. *Amer. J. Sociol.*, 1961, *66*, 335–341.
55. Perrow, C. Reality adjustment: A young institution settles for humane care. *Social Probl.*, 1966, *14*, 69–79.
56. Perrow, C. A framework for the comparative analysis of organizations. *Amer. Sociol. Rev.*, 1967, *32*, 194–208.
57. Perrow, C. Technology and organizational structure. *Proceedings of the nineteenth annual meeting of the Industrial Relations Research Association*. Madison, Wis.: 1967, 156–163.
58. Perrow, C. Technology and structural changes in business firms. In Roberts, B. C. (Ed.), *Industrial relations: Contemporary issues*. New York: Macmillan, 1968.
59. Perrow, C. *Complex organizations*. Chicago: Scott, Foresman, 1970.
60. Pinching 500,000,000 pennies. *Fortune*, 1963 (March).
61. Rice, A. K. *Productivity and social organization—The Ahmedabad experiment*. London: Tavistock, 1958.
62. Rieser, C. The chief shows them how at Indian Head. *Fortune*, 1962 (May).

63. Riesman, D. *The lonely crowd*. New Haven, Conn.: Yale Univ. Press, 1950.

64. Rosenthal, R. *Experimenter effects in behavioral research*. New York: Appleton-Century-Crofts, 1966.

65. Ross, I. The private turbulence of Eastern Air Lines. *Fortune*, 1964 (July).

66. Schumpeter, J. *Capitalism, socialism and democracy*. New York: Harper, 1942.

67. Scott, R. I. The selection of clients by social welfare agencies: The case of the blind. *Social Probl.*, 1967, *14*, 248–257.

68. Selznick, P. *TVA and the grass roots*. Berkeley, Calif.: Univ. of California Press, 1949.

69. Selznick, P. *Leadership in administration*. New York: Harper, 1957.

70. Sheehan, R. Daimler-Benz: Quality über alles. *Fortune*, 1961 (Aug.).

71. Sheehan, R. Great day in the morning for Texas Gulf Sulpher. *Fortune*, 1964 (July).

72. Sheehan, R. Proprietors in the world of big business. *Fortune*, 1967 (July).

73. Siekman, P. Henry Ford and his electronic can of worms. *Fortune*, 1955 (Feb.).

74. Sills, D. *The Volunteers: Means and ends in a national organization*. New York: The Free Press, 1957.

75. Simon, H. A. *Administrative behavior*. New York: Macmillan, 1947.

76. Skinner, B. F. Pigeons in a pelican. *Amer. Psychologist*, 1960, *15*, 28–37.

77. Smith, R. A. High stakes on the high seas. *Fortune*, 1961 (Oct.).

78. Street, D., Vinter, R., and Perrow, C. *Organization for treatment*. New York: The Free Press, 1966.

79. Tannenbaum, A., and Seashore, S. *Some changing conceptions and approaches to the study of persons in organizations*. Institute for Social Research, Univ. of Michigan. Mimeo., no date.

80. Thompson, J. D. *Organizations in action*. New York: McGraw-Hill, 1967.

81. Thompson, J. D., and McEwen, W. J. Organizational goals and environment. *Amer. Sociol. Rev.*, 1958, 23, 23–30.

82. Thompson, V. A. Bureaucracy and innovation. *Admin. Sci. Quart.*, 1965, *10*, 1–20.

83. Trist, E. L., and Bamforth, E. K. Some social and psychological consequences of the longwall method of coal-getting. *Hum. Rel.*, 1951, *4*, 3–38.

84. Turner, A., and Lawrence, P. *Industrial jobs and the worker.* Cambridge, Mass.: Harvard Univ. Press, 1965.
85. Verhave, T. The pigeon as a quality-control inspector. In Ulrich, R., Stachnik, T., and Mabry, J. (Eds.), *Control of human behavior.* Chicago: Scott, Foresman, 1966.
86. Waldo, D. *The administrative state.* New York: Ronald, 1948.
87. Walton, C. C. *Corporate social responsibility.* Belmont, Calif.: Wadsworth, 1967.
88. Weber, M. *The Protestant ethic and the spirit of capitalism.* Trans. by T. Parsons. New York: Scribner's, 1930.
89. Weber, M. *The theory of social and economic organization.* Trans. by T. Parsons. New York: The Free Press, 1947.
90. Weber, M. *Economy and society.* G. Roth and C. Wittich (Eds.). New York: Bedminster, 1968.
91. Whalen, R. J. The unoriginal ideas that rebuilt Crown Cork. *Fortune,* 1962 (Oct.).
92. Whalen, R. J. The durable threads of J. P. Stevens. *Fortune,* 1963 (April).
93. Wilensky, H. L. *Organization intelligence: Knowledge and policy in government and industry.* New York: Basic Books, 1967.
94. Woodward, J. *Industrial organization.* London: Oxford Univ. Press, 1965.

index

187

Republic Steel, 122
Reynolds Metals, 121
Rickenbacker, Eddie, 147–150, 159
Rieser, Carl, 163
Riesman, David, 3
Risk, 145–146, 152
Robinson, James E., 163–165
Rosenthal, Robert, 24
Routine and nonroutine tasks and technologies
  mixing tasks in organizations, 68–74
  routine and nonroutine tasks, 19–20, 35–36, 48–49, 63, 119–120, 178–179
  variability and search as aspects of, 75–85
Routinization, 67, 179
Rules and regulations
  absence of, 30–31, 42–43, 61, 70
  function of, 52–59
  presence of, 29–30, 40–41, 70

Sales domination, 8–11, 88
Sales versus production, 22–23, 87
Schools, 73–74, 79
Schumpeter, Joseph, 69, 130, 150
Scientific-management school, 14, 18–20, 42, 85
Scott, Robert I., 128
Sears, 172
Seashore, Stanley, 6–7
Secrecy, 125
Selznick, Philip, 8, 63–64, 113, 167, 173, 181
Senator Kefauver, 100
Sheehan, Robert, 152
Shipping industry (marine), 157
Siegel, Abraham, 115
Siekman, Philip, 139
Sills, David, 136
Simon, Herbert, 17, 27
Skinner, B. F., 119, 120
Sloan, Alfred, 153
Smith, Richard Austin, 157n

Snyderman, Barbara, 176
Social-psychological perspectives (see Sociological perspective; Structure of organizations)
Social responsibility of business, 101–104, 112, 139
Social welfare organizations, 132, 141
  agencies for the blind, 128
  psychiatric agency, 66–67, 79
  public welfare agencies, 127–130
  social agencies, 146
  welfare industry, 132
Socialism, 138–139
Sociological perspective, 21–26, 93–94
  attitudes and behavior, 24–25
  and the obvious, 94
  as "value free," 23
Socio-technical school, 20
Span of control, 15, 18–19, 63, 86
Specialization, 51ff., 178–179
Sporn, Philip, 156
Stability, 40–41, 56–59, 179
  as a system goal, 145–146, 152, 179
Staff specialists, 52–55, 57, 59
Stalker, G. M., 37, 45n
Stauffer, Robert E., 63
Stephens, Claude, 151–152
Stevens, J. P., 161–165
Street, David, 32
Structure of organizations, 10, 176–179
  structural explanations, 22–23
  structure and technology, 22–23
  structural view as distinguishing types of organizations, 27, 28
  structural viewpoint, 2, 7, 20, 175
Supervision, 6–7
Supreme Court, 157
Surgeon General's Office, 99
Susquehanna Corporation, 105
Sward, Keith, 64n
System goals, 144–158, 162–163